Financial Report Survey
March 1992

A15044 772305

# Illustrations of the Disclosure by Financial Institutions of Certain Information About Debt Securities Held as Assets

A Survey of the Application of SOP 90-11

Leonard Lorensen, CPA

American Institute of Certified Public Accountants

Copyright © 1992 by the
American Institute of Certified Public Accountants, Inc.
1211 Avenue of the Americas, New York, New York 10036-8775

1 2 3 4 5 6 7 8 9 0 IR 9 9 8 7 6 5 4 3 2

Library of Congress Cataloging-in-Publication Data

Lorensen, Leonard.
    Illustrations of the disclosure by financial institutions
of certain information about debt securities held as assets :
a survey of the application of SOP 90-11 / Leonard Lorensen.
        p.  cm. — (Financial report survey ; )
    "March 1992."
    ISBN 0-87051-122-X
        1.  Financial institutions—United States—Accounting.
2.  Financial statements—United States.  I.  American Institute
of Certified Public Accountants.  II.  Title.  III.  Series.
HG181.L67   1992
657' .833303—dc20                           92-21816
                                            CIP

# PREFACE

This publication is part of a series produced by the Institute's staff through use of the Institute's National Automated Accounting Research System (NAARS). The purpose of the series is to provide interested readers with examples of the application of technical pronouncements. It is believed that those who are confronted with problems in the application of pronouncements can benefit from seeing how others apply them in practice.

It is the intention to publish periodically similar compilations of information of current interest dealing with aspects of financial reporting.

The examples presented were selected from over twenty thousand annual reports stored in the NAARS computer data base.

This compilation presents only a limited number of examples and is not intended to encompass all aspects of the application of the pronouncements covered in this survey. Individuals with special application problems not illustrated in the survey may arrange for special computer searches of the NAARS data banks by contacting the Institute.

The views expressed are solely those of the staff.

Richard D. Walker
Director, Information Technology

# TABLE OF CONTENTS

# I

## SCOPE AND PURPOSE OF THE SURVEY

This survey is primarily intended to help accountants and auditors apply a pronouncement recently issued by the AICPA Accounting Standards Division, Statement of Position (SOP) 90-11, *Disclosure of Certain Information by Financial Institutions About Debt Securities Held as Assets.* SOP 90-11 is effective for financial statements for years ending after December 15, 1990.

Most financial institutions state debt securities held as assets at historical cost or the lower of cost or market value. SOP 90-11 requires this information to be disclosed in financial statement notes for each kind of securities stated on that basis: amortized cost, estimated market value, gross unrealized gains, gross unrealized losses, proceeds from sales, gross realized gains, and gross realized losses. In addition, amortized cost and estimated market value must be classified according to the various periods in which the securities will become due.

Disclosure of that information about debt securities in accordance with SOP 90-11 requires considerable judgment. An accountant or auditor who is confronted with problems in applying the pronouncement can benefit from learning how others have applied it in practice. Accordingly, this survey presents excerpts from recently published annual reports of fifty-six enterprises that illustrate the application of the pronouncement.

The AICPA National Automated Accounting Research System (NAARS) was used to compile the information. The examples presented were selected from the financial statements of fifty-six companies stored in the 1990-1991 annual report file. The search frame that was used is presented in the appendix.

# II

# BANKS

Banks are the most common kind of financial enterprises that present information about debt securities in accordance with SOP 90-11. Examples of information disclosed in accordance with SOP 90-11 by twenty-seven enterprises that operate primarily in the field of banking are presented below. The examples are classified according to which of these types of banks is the primary component of the disclosing enterprise:

● National commercial banks

● State commercial banks

● Savings institutions, federally chartered

● Savings institutions, state chartered

## NATIONAL COMMERCIAL BANKS

FIRST BANK SYSTEM INC., DECEMBER 31, 1990

*First Bank System, Inc. and Subsidiaries*
*Notes to Consolidated Financial Statements*

December 31, 1990

Note A—Significant Accounting Policies

●●●●

Securities - Investment securities which are held for long-term investment are stated at cost, as adjusted for accretion of discounts or amortization of premiums, computed by the interest method. The adjusted cost of the specific security sold is used to compute the gains or losses on the sale.

Securities held for sale are stated at the lower of cost or market value. Losses on the adjustments to market values are included in investment securities gains (losses).

•••

Note C—Investment Securities

The detail of the carrying amount, market value and gross unrealized appreciation and depreciation of investment securities at December 31 was as follows:

| (in millions) | Carrying Amount | Market Value | Gross Unrealized Appreciation | Gross Unrealized Depreciation |
|---|---|---|---|---|
| **1990** | | | | |
| United States Treasury | $ 578 | $ 578 | $ 3 | $ 3 |
| United States Government agencies | 502 | 486 | — | 16 |
| State and political subdivisions | 370 | 379 | 10 | 1 |
| Other | | 330 | 329 | 12 |
| Total | $1,780 | $1,772 | $ 14 | $22 |
| Securities held for sale | $ — | $ — | $ — | $— |
| **1989** | | | | |
| United States Treasury | $ 592 | $ 584 | $ — | $ 8 |
| United States Government agencies | 561 | 536 | 1 | 26 |
| State and political subdivisions | 427 | 439 | 19 | 7 |
| Other | 404 | 406 | 3 | 1 |
| Total | $1,984 | $1,965 | $ 23 | $42 |
| Securities held for sale | $ 425 | $ 425 | $ — | $— |

•••

Gross realized gains and losses on investment securities for the years ended December 31 were as follows:

| (in millions) | 1990 | 1989 | 1988 |
|---|---|---|---|
| Gross realized gains | $ .3 | $ 17.1 | $ 21.7 |
| Gross realized losses | (.1) | (1.1) | (519.1) |
| Net gains (losses) | $ .2 | $ 16.0 | $(497.4) |

•••

FIRST FLORIDA BANKS INC., DECEMBER 31, 1990

Notes

Note 1: Summary of Significant Accounting Policies

••••

Investment Securities

Investment securities, except for marketable equity securities, are stated at cost, adjusted for amortization of premiums and for accretion of discounts....

Gains or losses from the sales of investment securities are recognized upon realization based on the adjusted cost of each specific security and are included in the accompanying statements of operations.

••••

Note 4: Investment Securities

Investment securities are summarized below:

| (dollars in thousands) | December 31, 1990 | | December 31, 1989 | |
| --- | --- | --- | --- | --- |
| | Book Value | Market Value | Book Value | Market Value |
| United States Treasury securities | $257,608 | $263,020 | $180,231 | $181,512 |
| Securities of other U.S. Government agencies | 50,834 | 51,694 | 51,857 | 53,183 |
| Obligations of states and political subdivisions | 348,787 | 364,723 | 458,107 | 472,663 |
| ••••| | | | |
| Total | $669,240 | $691,391 | $711,652 | $726,734 |

••••

At December 31, 1990, gross unrealized gains on total investment securities with a carrying value of $669.2 million, totaled $26.6 million, and gross unrealized losses totaled $5.8 million. Gross realized gains on investment securities totaled $1.1 million for 1990, and gross realized losses totaled $152,000 for 1990.

As part of the Company's income tax strategy, certain obligations of states and political subdivisions with an aggregate net book value of $61.0 million were sold for $61.9 million in December of 1990. Similarly, certain such securities with an aggregate net book value of $49.6 million were sold for $51.0 million in January of 1991. The Company has the ability and the intent to hold all securities in its investment portfolio for the foreseeable future. However, certain investments in states and political subdivisions may be sold in conjunction with tax planning strategies.

The amortized cost and estimated market values of investments in debt securities were as follows at December 31, 1990.

| (*dollars in thousands*) | Amortized Cost | Gross Unrealized Losses | Gross Unrealized Gains | Estimated Market Value |
|---|---|---|---|---|
| United States Treasury securities and obligations of U.S. Government corporations and agencies | $308,442 | $ 6,531 | $ (259) | $314,714 |
| Obligations of states and political subdivisions | 348,787 | 19,956 | (4,020) | 364,723 |
| Debt securities issued by foreign governments | 179 | — | (3) | 176 |
| Corporate securities | 5,577 | 65 | (119) | 5,523 |
| Mortgage-backed securities | 213,234 | 1,622 | (287) | 214,569 |
| Totals | $876,219 | $28,174 | $(4,688) | $899,705 |

The amortized cost and estimated market value of debt securities at December 31, 1990, by contractual maturity, are shown below. Expected maturities will differ from contractual maturities because borrowers may have the right to call or prepay obligations with or without call or prepayment penalties.

| | Amortized Cost | Estimated Market Value |
|---|---|---|
| Due in one year or less | $128,571 | $129,094 |
| Due after one year through five years | 319,204 | 328,175 |
| Due after five years through ten years | 160,494 | 170,110 |
| Due after ten years | 54,716 | 57,757 |
| Mortgage-backed securities | 213,234 | 214,569 |
| | $876,219 | $899,705 |

Proceeds from sales of investments in debt securities during 1990 were $132.6 million. Gross gains of $1.1 million and gross losses of $152,000 were realized on those sales.

FIRST INTERSTATE BANCORP, DECEMBER 31, 1990

Notes to Financial Statements

Note A—Accounting Policies

• • • •

Securities

The Corporation reviews its financial position, liquidity and future plans in evaluating the criteria for classifying investment securities. Generally, securities are classified between investment and trading at the time the securities are purchased. Securities in the investment account are stated at cost, increased by accretion of discounts and reduced by amortization of premiums, both computed by the straight-line method, which does not differ materially from the interest method. The adjusted cost of specific securities sold is used to compute gains or losses on securities transactions. Trading account securities are carried at market value. Gains and losses, both realized and unrealized, are included in noninterest income. Securities identified and held for sale are separately classified, and are valued at the lower of cost or market. Market values of securities are estimated based on available market quotations. In the few instances when market quotations are unavailable, the securities are stated at cost or appraised values as deemed appropriate by management.

• • • •

Note B—Investment Securities

A comparison of the carrying amount, approximate market value of investment securities and gross unrealized gains and losses on such securities follows (*in thousands*):

| | Carrying Amount | Approximate Market Value | Gross Gains | Unrealized Losses |
|---|---|---|---|---|
| **December 31, 1990:** | | | | |
| U.S. Treasury securities | $1,313,512 | $1,339,605 | $ 26,672 | $    579 |
| U.S. government agency securities: | | | | |
| Mortgage-backed securities | 2,916,194 | 2,945,544 | 49,706 | 20,356 |
| Other agencies | 508,104 | 516,028 | 8,210 | 286 |
| State and political subdivisions: | 704,302 | 707,716 | 10,611 | 7,197 |
| Mortgage-backed securities | 795,058 | 804,327 | 9,593 | 324 |
| Other debt securities | 339,308 | 341,967 | 3,549 | 890 |
| Corporate and Federal Reserve Bank stock | 90,507 | 92,367 | 1,860 | — |
| Total Investment Securities | $6,666,985 | $6,747,554 | $110,201 | $29,632 |
| Securities held for sale | $  308,080 | $  313,704 | $  5,624 | $     — |
| **December 31, 1989:** | | | | |
| U.S. Treasury securities | $1,941,877 | $1,968,478 | $ 27,698 | $ 1,097 |
| U.S. government agency securities: | | | | |
| Mortgage-backed securities | 2,336,778 | 2,341,979 | 23,615 | 18,414 |
| Other agencies | 226,726 | 231,178 | 4,986 | 534 |
| State and political subdivisions: | 1,189,122 | 1,194,373 | 23,040 | 17,789 |
| Mortgage-backed securities | 1,225,479 | 1,236,346 | 12,414 | 1,547 |
| Other debt securities | 664,937 | 670,483 | 6,686 | 1,140 |
| Corporate and Federal Reserve Bank stock | 111,207 | 127,903 | 16,696 | — |
| Total Investment Securities | $7,696,126 | $7,770,740 | $115,135 | $40,521 |

Maturities of debt securities classified as investments as of December 31, 1990 are as follows (*in thousands*):

|  | Carrying Amount | Approximate Market Value |
|---|---|---|
| Due in one year or less | $1,075,437 | $1,079,626 |
| Due after one year through five years | 2,043,715 | 2,049,248 |
| Due after five years through ten years | 485,547 | 442,518 |
| Due after ten years | 2,971,779 | 3,083,795 |
| Total | $6,576,478 | $6,655,187 |

Maturities of mortgage-backed securities are classified in accordance with the contractual repayment schedules. Expected maturities differ from the contractual maturities reported above because debt security issuers may have the right to call or repay obligations with or without call or prepayments penalties.

•••

Proceeds from sales of investment securities during 1990 were $758.7 million. Gross gains of $13.9 million and gross losses of $3.3 million were realized on those sales.

FIRST NATIONAL CORPORATION, DECEMBER 31, 1990

*Notes To Consolidated Financial Statements*

(1) Summary of Significant Accounting Policies:

•••

(b) Investment Securities:

Investment securities are stated at cost, adjusted for amortization of premiums and accretion of discounts. Realized gains and losses on the sale of investment securities are determined using the adjusted costs of the specific securities sold. The Bank intends to hold investment securities until maturity and accordingly, no adjustments are made for securities whose book value exceeds market value.

•••

(2) Investment Securities:

The book value and approximate market value of investment securities as of December 31, 1990 and 1989 are as follows:

|  | 1990 | | 1989 | |
|---|---|---|---|---|
|  | Book Value | Approximate Market Value | Book Value | Approximate Market Value |
|  | *(dollars in thousands)* | | | |
| U.S. Treasury and other U.S. government agencies and corporations | $ 8,552 | $ 8,632 | $ 7,354 | $ 7,360 |

|  | 1990 | | 1989 | |
| --- | --- | --- | --- | --- |
|  | Book Value | Approximate Market Value | Book Value | Approximate Market Value |
|  | *(dollars in thousands)* | | | |
| Obligations of states and political subdivisions | 745 | 744 | 2,153 | 2,154 |
| Federal Reserve Bank stock | 725 | 725 | 725 | 725 |
|  | $10,022 | $10,101 | $10,232 | $10,239 |

At December 31, 1990, gross unrealized losses and gross unrealized gains were $1,000 and $80,000, respectively. At December 31, 1989, gross unrealized losses and gross unrealized gains were $10,000 and $17,000, respectively. None of the Bank's investment securities are held for trading purposes.

The maturity distribution based on book value (which approximates market value) of the investment portfolio (excluding Federal Reserve Bank stock) at December 31, 1990 is as follows:

|  | Maturity Distribution | | |
| --- | --- | --- | --- |
| *(dollars in thousands)* | Within One Year | One to Five Years | Total |
| U.S. Treasury and other U.S. government agencies and corporations | $6,604 | $1,948 | $8,552 |
| Obligations of states and political subdivisions | 300 | 445 | 745 |
|  | $6,904 | $2,393 | $9,297 |

● ● ● ●

FIRST TENNESSEE NATIONAL CORPORATION, DECEMBER 31, 1990

*Notes to Consolidated Financial Statements*

Note 1—Summary of Significant Accounting Policies

● ● ● ●

Investment securities

Investment securities include both debt and equity securities. The Corporation has both the intent and ability to carry these securities into the foreseeable future. Debt securities are carried at cost, adjusted for amortization of premiums and accretion of discounts, which are recognized as adjustments to interest income. Gains and losses on the sale of debt securities are computed by the specific identification method and are included in noninterest income.

● ● ● ●

Note 5—Investment Securities

● ● ● ●

The book value and related market value of investment securities at December 31 are presented below:

| (*thousands*) | 1990 | 1989 |
|---|---|---|
| **Book Value:** | | |
| U.S. Treasury and other | | |
| U.S. government agencies | $1,041,323 | $ 979,990 |
| States and political subdivisions | 150,767 | 197,037 |
| Other | 212,097 | 148,465 |
| Equity | 13,226 | 16,776 |
| Total | $1,417,413 | $1,342,268 |
| **Market Value:** | | |
| U.S. Treasury and other | | |
| U.S. government agencies | $1,050,593 | $ 982,079 |
| States and political subdivisions | 154,579 | 201,714 |
| Other | 208,477 | 143,673 |
| Equity | 12,252 | 18,871 |
| Total | $1,425,901 | $1,346,337 |

A reconciliation of the amortized cost to the estimated market values of investments in securities at December 31, 1990, is presented below:

| (*thousands*) | Amortized Cost | Gross Unrealized Gains | Gross Unrealized Losses | Estimated Market Value |
|---|---|---|---|---|
| U.S. Treasury and other U.S. government agencies | $ 354,008 | $ 5,642 | $ (5) | $ 359,645 |
| States and political subdivisions | 150,767 | 5,161 | (1,349) | 154,579 |
| Corporate | 240 | 12 | — | 252 |
| Mortgage-backed | 691,354 | 7,714 | (4,060) | 695,008 |
| Other | 207,818 | 679 | (4,332) | 204,165 |
| Equity | 13,226 | 87 | (1,061) | 12,252 |
| Total | $1,417,413 | $19,295 | $(10,807) | $1,425,901 |

The amortized cost and estimated market value of securities at December 31, 1990, by contractual maturity, are shown below. Expected maturities will differ from contractual maturities because borrowers may have the right to call or prepay obligations with or without call or prepayment penalties.

| (*thousands*) | Amortized Cost | Estimated Market Value |
|---|---|---|
| 0-1 year | $ 197,309 | $ 198,945 |
| 1-5 years | 359,427 | 366,869 |
| 5-10 years | 33,816 | 34,270 |
| Over 10 years | 122,281 | 118,557 |

| (*thousands*) | Amortized Cost | Estimated Market Value |
|---|---|---|
| Subtotal | 712,833 | 718,641 |
| Mortgage-backed securities | 691,354 | 695,008 |
| Equity securities | 13,226 | 12,252 |
| Total | $1,417,413 | $1,425,901 |

Proceeds from sales of investments in debt securities during 1990 were $309,099,000. Gross gains of $1,102,000 and gross losses of $1,060,000 were realized on those sales.

Net investment debt securities gains (losses) after taxes were ($589,000), ($139,000), and $115,000, for the years ended December 31, 1990, 1989, and 1988, respectively. The applicable income tax expenses (benefits) were ($360,000), ($85,000), and $71,000 for the years ended December 31, 1990, 1989, and 1988, respectively.

Included in investment debt securities losses for 1990 is a loss in value of $998,000 for securities that in the opinion of management have been permanently impaired.


FIRST UNION CORPORATION, DECEMBER 31, 1990

*Notes to Consolidated Financial Statements*
*First Union Corporation and Subsidiaries*
*(December 31, 1990, 1989 and 1988)*

Note 1: Summary of Significant Accounting and Reporting Policies

• • • •

Trading Account Assets and Investment Securities

• • • •

Investment securities, primarily debt securities, are stated at cost, net of the amortization of premium and the accretion of discount, when the Corporation has the ability and intent to hold such securities to maturity. Prior to their maturity, the Corporation may sell investment securities if it determines under then prevailing and projected economic conditions that such sales would be a safe and sound banking practice and in the best interest of the stockholders of the Corporation. Investment securities designated to be sold are recorded at the lower of cost or market value and are classified separately in the financial statements of the Corporation when appropriate.

Gains or losses on the sale of investment securities are recognized on a specific identification, trade date basis.

• • • •

Note 3: Investment Securities

| | 1990 | | | | |
|---|---|---|---|---|---|
| (*in thousands*) | 1 Year or Less | 1-5 Years | 5-10 Years | After 10 Years | Total |
| Carrying Values | | | | | |
| U.S. Treasury | $ 1,656 | 1,618,528 | 3,016 | — | 1,623,200 |

*Investment Securities (continued)*

| (*in thousands*) | 1990 | | | | |
|---|---|---|---|---|---|
| | 1 Year or Less | 1-5 Years | 5-10 Years | After 10 Years | Total |
| U.S. Government agencies | 52,390 | 186,408 | 693,667 | 2,381,424 | 3,313,889 |
| State, county and municipal | 47,548 | 385,231 | 239,072 | 908,929 | 1,580,780 |
| Other | 7,761 | 1,037,854 | 194,652 | 296,691 | 1,536,958 |
| Total | $109,355 | 3,228,021 | 1,130,407 | 3,587,044 | 8,054,827 |
| | | | | | |
| Carrying values | | | | | |
| Debt securities | $102,939 | 3,228,021 | 1,129,938 | 3,302,554 | 7,763,452 |
| Sundry securities | 6,416 | — | 469 | 284,490 | 291,375 |
| Total | $109,355 | 3,228,021 | 1,130,407 | 3,587,044 | 8,054,827 |
| | | | | | |
| Market Values | | | | | |
| Debt securities | $103,585 | 3,277,243 | 1,137,590 | 3,306,943 | 7,825,361 |
| Sundry securities | 6,416 | — | 469 | 258,508 | 265,393 |
| Total | $110,001 | 3,277,243 | 1,138,059 | 3,565,451 | 8,090,754 |

| (*in thousands*) | 1990 | | | 1989 | |
|---|---|---|---|---|---|
| | Gross Gains | Unrealized Losses | Market Value | Carrying Value | Market Value |
| Carrying Values | | | | | |
| U.S. Treasury | 19,955 | (23) | 1,643,132 | 55,270 | 55,814 |
| U.S. Government agencies | 21,151 | (61,656) | 3,273,38 | 3,560,830 | 3,482,321 |
| State, county and municipal | 109,757 | (7,944) | 1,682,593 | 1,638,599 | 1,768,085 |
| Other | 9,985 | (55,298) | 1,491,645 | 865,633 | 832,113 |
| Total | 160,848 | (124,921) | 8,090,754 | 6,120,332 | 6,138,333 |
| | | | | | |
| Carrying Values | | | | | |
| Debt securities | 160,391 | (98,482) | 7,825,361 | | |
| Sundry securities | 457 | (26,439) | 265,393 | | |
| Total | 160,848 | (124,921) | 8,090,754 | | |

●●●●

Included in "Other" at December 31, 1990, are $779,982,000 of primarily U.S. Government agency collateralized mortgage obligations with a market value of $789,007,000.

Expected maturities differ from contractual maturities since borrowers may have the right to call or repay obligations with or without call or prepayment penalties. The aging of mortgage-backed securities is based on their weighted average maturities at December 31, 1990.

Gross gains and losses realized on the sale of debt securities during 1990 were $29,867,000 and $21,069,000, respectively, and on sundry securities were $117,000 and $67,000, respectively.

*First Wachovia Corporation and Subsidiaries*
*Notes to Consolidated Financial Statements*
*$ in thousands*

Note A—Accounting Policies

•••

Investment Securities - Investment securities are acquired with the intent and ability to hold on a long-term basis and are carried at cost adjusted for amortization of premium and accretion of discount, both computed by the interest method. The adjusted cost of the specific security sold is used to compute gains or losses on the sale of investment securities. Investment securities are concentrated in a variety of state and municipal, U.S. Treasury and federal agency obligations.

Trading Account Assets - Trading account assets are held with the intent of selling them at a profit and are carried at market.

•••

Note B—Investment Securities

The aggregate book and market values of investment securities as of December 31, 1990 and 1989 as well as gross unrealized gains and losses of investment securities as of December 31, 1990 were as follows:

|  | 1990 | | |
|---|---|---|---|
|  | Book Value | Unrealized Gains | Unrealized Losses |
| State and municipal | $ 737,647 | $ 62,533 | $ (1,491) |
| United States Treasury | 911,814 | 36,022 | (450) |
| Federal agency | 1,342,586 | 24,704 | (7,032) |
| Other | 787,076 | 6,741 | (1,858) |
| Total investment securities | $3,779,123 | $130,000 | ($10,831) |

|  | 1990 Market Value | Book Value | 1989 Market Value |
|---|---|---|---|
| State and municipal | $ 798,689 | $ 788,602 | $ 858,005 |
| United States Treasury | 947,386 | 1,029,225 | 1,062,749 |
| Federal agency | 1,360,258 | 969,505 | 972,688 |
| Other | 791,959 | 811,049 | 818,860 |
| Total investment securities | $3,898,292 | $3,598,381 | $3,712,302 |

Included in gross unrealized gains and losses are unrealized gains of $5,956 and losses of $56 related to nondebt securities.

The amortized cost and estimated market value of investment securities at December 31, 1990, by contractual maturity, are shown below. Expected maturities may differ from contractual maturities because borrowers may have the right to call or prepay obligations with or without call or prepayment penalties.

|                                        | Book Value | Market Value |
|----------------------------------------|-----------:|-------------:|
| Due in one year or less                | $ 256,851  | $ 258,380    |
| Due after one year through five years  | 1,017,349  | 1,042,471    |
| Due after five years through ten years | 929,486    | 968,770      |
| Due after ten years                    | 1,556,678  | 1,604,013    |
| Total                                  | 3,760,364  | 3,873,634    |
| No contractual maturity                | 18,759     | 24,658       |
| Total investment securities            | $3,779,123 | $3,898,292   |

Proceeds from sales of investments in debt securities during 1990 were $259,462. Gross gains of $1,249 and gross losses of $367 were realized on those sales. The gross proceeds and gross gains from the sales of nondebt securities totaled $6,219 and $5,346, respectively.

•••• 

# STATE COMMERCIAL BANKS

AMSOUTH BANCORPORATION, DECEMBER 31, 1990

*Notes to Consolidated Financial Statements*
*AmSouth Bancorporation and Subsidiaries*
*Years Ended December 31, 1990, 1989 and 1988*

Note A

Summary of Significant Accounting Policies

•••• 

Investment Securities

Investment securities are securities purchased with the intent and ability to hold for the foreseeable future. Investment securities are stated at cost, adjusted for amortization of premiums and accretion of discounts on the straight-line method. The adjusted cost of the specific certificate sold is used to compute gains or losses on the sale of investment securities.

•••• 

Note C

Investment Securities

The amounts at which investment securities are carried and their approximate fair market values are summarized as follows:

| December 31 (*in thousands*) | 1990 | | 1989 | |
|---|---|---|---|---|
| | Carrying Amount | Market Value | Carrying Amount | Market Value |
| U.S. Treasury and Federal agency securities | $1,330,618 | $1,341,741 | $1,328,831 | $1,327,132 |

14

| December 31 (in thousands) | 1990 | | 1989 | |
|---|---|---|---|---|
| | Carrying Amount | Market Value | Carrying Amount | Market Value |
| State, county and municipal obligations | 478,391 | 485,492 | 487,175 | 493,220 |
| Other Securities | 164,949 | 165,272 | 135,403 | 135,111 |
| | $1,973,958 | $1,992,505 | $1,951,409 | $1,955,463 |

The carrying amount, gross unrealized gains/losses and the approximate market value of investment securities are as follows. Amounts shown for U.S. Treasury and Federal agency securities and other securities do not agree with the above table because of the reclassification of mortgage-backed securities.

| December 31, 1990 (in thousands) | Carrying Amount | Gross Unrealized Gains | Gross Unrealized Losses | Market Value |
|---|---|---|---|---|
| U.S. Treasury and Federal agency securities | $ 271,525 | $ 1,499 | $1,713 | $ 271,311 |
| State, county and municipal obligations | 478,391 | 11,567 | 4,466 | 485,492 |
| Mortgage-backed securities | 1,206,945 | 12,703 | 1,023 | 1,218,625 |
| Other Securities | 17,097 | 0 | 20 | 17,077 |
| | $1,973,958 | $25,769 | $7,222 | $1,992,505 |

The carrying amount and approximate market value of investment securities by maturity were as follows:

| December 31 (in thousands) | 1990 | |
|---|---|---|
| | Carrying Amount | Market Value |
| Due in one year or less | $ 98,825 | $ 98,601 |
| Due after 1 year through 5 years | 311,164 | 312,940 |
| Due after 5 years through 10 years | 138,156 | 140,108 |
| Due after ten years | 218,868 | 222,231 |
| Mortgage-backed securities | 1,206,945 | 1,218,625 |
| | $1,973,958 | $1,992,505 |

Proceeds from sales of investment securities during 1990 were $175,214,000. Gross gains of $588,000 and gross losses of $162,000 were realized on those sales.

•   •   •   •

BANKERS TRUST NEW YORK CORPORATION, DECEMBER 31, 1990

*Bankers Trust New York Corporation and Subsidiaries (Consolidated)*
*And Bankers Trust Company and Subsidiaries (Consolidated)*
*Notes to Financial Statements*

Note 1—Significant Accounting Policies

••••

Investment Securities, Trading Account Assets and Securities Sold, Not Yet Purchased

The Corporation generally designates securities as either trading account assets or investment securities at the date of acquisition.

Debt investment securities are carried at cost, adjusted for amortization of premiums and accretion of discounts. The Corporation has the ability to hold these securities to maturity and it intends to hold such securities for the foreseeable future.... The specific identification method is used to determine the cost of investment securities sold.

••••

Note 3—Investment Securities; Assets Pledged

The Corporation's investment securities' book value and market value (or estimated market value for certain investment securities where no market quotations were available) including gross unrealized gains and losses at December 31, 1990 follow:

| December 31, (in millions) | 1990 | | | |
|---|---|---|---|---|
| | Book Value | Gross Unrealized | | Market Value |
| | | Gains | (Losses) | |
| U.S. Treasury | $ 908 | $ 9 | $(10) | $ 907 |
| U.S. government agencies and corporations | 1,443 | 19 | — | 1,462 |
| States and political subdivisions | 1,170 | 112 | (14) | 1,268 |
| Other bonds, notes, debentures and redeemable preferred stock | 3,407 | 15 | (33) | 3,389 |
| Federal Reserve Bank and other corporate stock | 102 | — | — | 102 |
| Total investment securities | $7,030 | $155 | $(57) | $7,128 |

| | 1989 | | 1988 | |
|---|---|---|---|---|
| | Book Value | Market Value | Book Value | Market Value |
| U.S. Treasury | $ 967 | $ 959 | $ 338 | $ 313 |
| U.S. government agencies and corporations | 1,544 | 1,550 | 255 | 247 |
| States and political subdivisions | 1,272 | 1,384 | 1,511 | 1,603 |
| Other bonds, notes, debentures and redeemable preferred stock | 2,642 | 2,629 | 2,185 | 2,183 |
| Federal Reserve Bank and other corporate stock | 122 | 156 | 39 | 39 |
| Total investment securities | $6,547 | $6,678 | $4,328 | $4,385 |

••••

As reported in the Corporation's consolidated statement of cash flows, the combined proceeds from redemptions and sales of investment securities, excluding short-term investment securities, were $9.398 billion and $6.147 billion for the years ended December 31, 1990 and 1989, respectively. The 1990 total consisted of $7.999 billion of proceeds from redemptions and $1.399

billion of proceeds from sales. Gross realized gains of $34 million and gross realized losses of $14 million from those 1990 sales were included in the consolidated statement of income. It is estimated that approximately one-third of the 1989 combined proceeds resulted from sales.

The following table shows the book value, remaining maturities, approximate weighted average yields (not on a fully taxable basis) and total market value by maturity distribution of the debt and redeemable preferred stock components of the Corporation's investment securities at December 31, 1990. The maturity distribution for mortgage-backed securities is based on the contractual due date of the final payment.

| | Maturity Distribution | | | |
| | Within One Year | | After One But Within Five Years | |
| ($ in millions) | Amount | Yield | Amount | Yield |
|---|---|---|---|---|
| U.S. Treasury | $ 97 | 7.4% | $ 20 | 10.4% |
| U.S. government agencies and corporations | — | — | 2 | 8.9 |
| States and political subdivisions | 4 | 5.7 | 493 | 8.9 |
| Other bonds, notes, debentures and redeemable preferred stock | 1,185 | 12.3 | 1,727 | 11.3 |
| Total book value | $1,286 | | $2,242 | |
| Total market value | $1,286 | | $2,225 | |

| | After Five But Within Ten Years | | After Ten Years | | Total | |
| | Amount | Yield | Amount | Yield | Amount | Yield |
|---|---|---|---|---|---|---|
| U.S. Treasury | $ 791 | 7.9% | $ — | —% | $ 908 | 7.9% |
| U.S. government agencies and corporations | 123 | 7.4 | 1,318 | 8.4 | 1,443 | 8.3 |
| States and political subdivisions | 90 | 8.9 | 583 | 8.4 | 1,170 | 8.7 |
| Other bonds, notes, debentures and redeemable preferred stock | 468 | 12.9 | 27 | 20.0 | 3,407 | 11.9 |
| Total book value | $1,472 | | $1,928 | | $6,928 | |
| Total market value | $1,531 | | $1,984 | | $7,026 | |

•• ••

FIRST EMPIRE STATE CORPORATION, DECEMBER 31, 1990

*Notes To Financial Statements*

1. Significant accounting policies

•• ••

Investment securities

Investment securities in the form of debt instruments are carried at cost, adjusted for the accretion of discounts and amortization of premiums, when management has both the ability and intent to hold these securities until maturity. Periodic sales of these securities occur principally as a result of reactive measures taken by management to changing business circumstances. When it becomes probable that a debt investment security will be sold, the Company carries the security at the lower-of-cost or fair market value.

....Gains or losses on the sales of all investment securities are determined using the specific identification method.

• • • •

3. Investment securities

The amortized cost and estimated market values of investment securities were as follows:

| (in thousands) | Amortized Cost | Gross Unrealized Gains | Gross Unrealized Losses | Estimated Market Value |
|---|---|---|---|---|
| **December 31, 1990** | | | | |
| U.S. Treasury and federal agency | $ 60,780 | 50 | 1,082 | 59,748 |
| Obligations of states and political subdivisions | 164,096 | 527 | 129 | 164,494 |
| Mortgage-backed securities | | | | |
| Government issued or guaranteed | 1,065,014 | 11,585 | 4,179 | 1,072,693 |
| Other | 97,583 | 1,236 | 21 | 98,798 |
| Other securities | 35,744 | 3,594 | 1,385 | 37,953 |
| Total | $1,423,217 | 17,265 | 6,796 | 1,433,686 |
| **December 31, 1989** | | | | |
| U.S. Treasury and federal agency | $ 156,656 | 38 | 2,790 | 153,904 |
| Obligations of states and political subdivisions | 100,777 | 151 | 883 | 100,045 |
| Mortgage-backed securities | | | | |
| Government issued or guaranteed | 780,756 | 6,886 | 1,968 | 785,674 |
| Other | 80,408 | 383 | — | 80,791 |
| Other securities | 18,053 | 4,721 | 597 | 22,177 |
| Total | $1,136,650 | 12,179 | 6,238 | 1,142,591 |

Included in other securities are equity securities amounting to $10,308,000 at December 31, 1990 and $11,111,000 at December 31, 1989.

The amortized cost and estimated market value of debt securities by contractual maturity were as follows:

| December 31, 1990 (in thousands) | Amortized Cost | Estimated Market Value |
|---|---|---|
| Due in one year or less | $ 167,652 | 168,027 |
| Due after one year through five years | 47,940 | 47,874 |
| Due after five years through ten years | 23,960 | 23,127 |

18

| December 31, 1990 (*in thousands*) | Amortized Cost | Estimated Market Value |
|---|---|---|
| Due after ten years | 10,760 | 10,632 |
|  | 250,312 | 249,660 |
| Mortgage-backed securities | 1,162,597 | 1,171,491 |
|  | $1,412,909 | 1,421,151 |

Included in mortgage-backed securities are collateralized mortgage obligations amounting to $321,239,000 at December 31, 1990 and $1,789,000 at December 31, 1989.

Proceeds from sales of investments in debt securities during 1990 were $131,987,000. Gross gains of $64,000 and gross losses of $1,333,000 were realized on those sales.

• • • •

FIRST ILLINOIS CORPORATION, DECEMBER 31, 1990

*First Illinois Corporation and Subsidiaries*
*Notes to Financial Statements*

Summary of Significant Accounting Policies

• • • •

Investment Securities

Debt securities held as investments are stated at net book value as it is management's intent to hold such securities until their scheduled maturities. Debt securities are periodically sold prior to maturity and replaced with similar debt securities of comparable par values to improve the Company's consolidated interest sensitivity position. Premiums on debt securities are amortized and discounts are accreted using the effective yield method.... Gains or losses on sales of investment securities are recorded on a completed transaction basis using the specific identification method.

• • • •

Investment Securities

The book and approximate market values of investment securities at December 31, 1990 are as follows:

| (*in thousands*) | Book Value | Gross Unrealized Gains | Gross Unrealized Losses | Market Value |
|---|---|---|---|---|
| U. S. Treasury | $102,215 | $1,576 | $(101) | $103,690 |
| U. S. Government Agency | 97,527 | 1,173 | (61) | 98,639 |
| States and Political Subdivisions | 109,260 | 3,253 | (117) | 112,386 |
| Other | 10,347 | 756 | (3) | 11,100 |
| Total | $319,349 | $6,758 | $(282) | $325,825 |

The book and approximate market values of investment securities at December 31, 1989 were as follows:

| (*in thousands*) | Book Value | Net Unrealized Gain | Market Value |
|---|---|---|---|
| U. S. Treasury | $128,580 | $1,004 | $129,584 |
| U. S. Government Agency | 60,538 | 390 | 60,928 |
| States and Political Subdivisions | 131,770 | 2,397 | 134,167 |
| Other | 8,876 | 517 | 9,393 |
| Total | $329,764 | $4,308 | $334,072 |

The following schedule summarizes the contractual maturities, by book value, and average taxable equivalent yields of investments in debt securities at December 31, 1990:

| (*dollars in thousands*) | U.S. Treasury | U.S. Government Agency | States and Political Subdivisions | Other | Average Taxable Equivalent Yield |
|---|---|---|---|---|---|
| One year or less | $ 43,394 | $17,607 | $ 25,089 | $1,091 | 9.10% |
| One year to five years | 56,877 | 71,879 | 60,614 | 4,627 | 9.06 |
| Five years to ten years | 967 | 3,176 | 19,018 | 100 | 10.23 |
| Over ten years | 977 | 4,865 | 4,539 | 1,004 | 9.22 |
| Total | $102,215 | $97,527 | $109,260 | $6,822 | 9.16% |
| Average Taxable Equivalent Yield | 8.68% | 8.74% | 10.26% | 4.89% | 9.16% |

The following schedule summarizes the contractual maturities, by market value, of investments in debt securities at December 31, 1990:

| (*in thousands*) | U.S. Treasury | U.S. Government Agency | States and Political Subdivisions | Other |
|---|---|---|---|---|
| One year or less | $ 43,731 | $17,693 | $ 25,208 | $1,093 |
| One year to five years | 58,099 | 72,869 | 42,419 | 4,651 |
| Five years to ten years | 973 | 3,179 | 20,042 | 100 |
| Over ten years | 887 | 4,898 | 4,727 | 1,731 |
| Total | $103,690 | $98,639 | $112,396 | $7,575 |

Actual maturities will differ from contractual maturities as security issuers may have the right to call or prepay obligations with or without call or prepayment penalties. In other instances, the Company may have the right to accelerate the repayment of obligations.

●●●●

Proceeds from sales of investment securities during 1990, 1989 and 1988 were $40,070,000, $25,381,000, and $10,168,000, respectively. Gross gains and gross losses of $85,000 and $(5,000), $366,000 and $(39,000), and $82,000 and $(3,000) were realized on those sales in 1990, 1989 and 1988, respectively.

●●●●

FIRST SECURITY CORPORATION, DECEMBER 31, 1990

*First Security Corporation & Subsidiaries*
*Notes to Consolidated Financial Statements*

Note 1. Summary of Significant Accounting and Reporting Policies

•••

Securities (See Note 3): .... Investment securities are carried at cost, plus discount accreted or less premium amortized, based on management's intent and the Corporation's and its subsidiaries' ability to hold such securities for the foreseeable future. The ability and intent are based on management's evaluation of liquidity requirements and asset/liability structure. Gains and losses are determined on the specific identification method.

•••

Note 3. Investment Securities

The amortized cost and estimated market values of investment securities are as follows (*in thousands*):

|  | Amortized Cost | Gross Unrealized Gains | Gross Unrealized Losses | Estimated Market Value |
|---|---|---|---|---|
| As of December 31, 1990 |  |  |  |  |
| U.S. Treasury and other U.S. Government agencies and corporations | $ 740,750 | $ 8,740 | $ (390) | $ 748,830 |
| Obligations of states and political subdivisions | 122,575 | 452 | (1,798) | 121,229 |
| Corporate securities | 143,366 | 909 | (810) | 143,465 |
| Equity securities | 13,326 | 520 | (97) | 13,749 |
| Totals | $1,020,017 | $10,351 | $(3,095) | $1,027,273 |
| As of December 31, 1989 |  |  |  |  |
| U.S. Treasury and other U.S. Government agencies and corporations | $ 702,565 | $ 2,796 | $ (796) | $ 704,565 |
| Obligations of states and political subdivisions | 114,907 | 500 | (2,425) | 112,982 |
| Corporate securities | 184,426 | 1,003 | (720) | 184,709 |
| Equity securities | 13,159 | 358 | (127) | 13,390 |
| Totals | $1,015,057 | $ 4,657 | $(4,068) | $1,015,646 |

The amortized cost and estimated market value of investment securities at December 31, 1990 by contractual maturity are shown below (in thousands). Expected maturities will differ from contractual maturities because borrowers may have the right to call or prepay obligations with or without call or prepayment penalties.

|  | Amortized Cost | Estimated Market Value |
|---|---|---|
| Due in one year or less | $ 327,110 | $ 329,342 |
| Due after one year through five years | 273,033 | 274,622 |
| Due after five years through ten years | 56,452 | 56,330 |
| Due after ten years | 350,096 | 353,230 |
| Total debt securities | 1,006,691 | 1,013,524 |
| Equity securities | 13,326 | 13,749 |
| Totals | $1,020,017 | $1,027,273 |

Proceeds, gross gains, and gross losses from sales of investments in securities are as follows (*in thousands*):

|  | 1990 | 1989 | 1988 |
|---|---|---|---|
| Proceeds | $1,189,858 | $554,007 | $1,046,342 |
| Gross gains | $ 973 | $ 1,179 | $ 985 |
| Gross losses | (445) | (872) | (1,068) |
| Net gains (losses) | $ 528 | $ 307 | $ (83) |

• • • •

FIRST VIRGINIA BANKS INC., DECEMBER 31, 1990

*Notes To Consolidated Financial Statements*

1. Summary Of Significant Accounting Policies

• • • •

Investment Securities

All securities are held for investment purposes. Debt securities are carried at cost, adjusted for amortization of premiums and accretion of discounts.... The adjusted carrying value of the specific security sold is used to compute gains or losses on the sale of investment securities.

• • • •

4. Investment Securities

The carrying amounts of investment securities and the related approximate market values were (*in thousands*):

|  | Carrying Amount | Unrealized Gains | Unrealized Losses | Market Value |
|---|---|---|---|---|
| December 31, 1990: |  |  |  |  |
| U.S. Government and its agencies | $ 949,824 | $13,320 | $ 91 | $ 963,053 |
| State and municipal obligations | 271,097 | 2,080 | 563 | 272,614 |
| Other | 65,860 | 1,742 | 1,000 | 66,602 |
|  | $1,286,781 | $17,142 | $1,654 | $1,302,269 |

|  | Carrying Amount | Unrealized Gains | Unrealized Losses | Market Value |
|---|---|---|---|---|
| December 31, 1989: | | | | |
| U.S. Government and its agencies | $ 762,583 | | | $ 767,028 |
| State and municipal obligations | 238,603 | | | 239,701 |
| Other | 67,896 | | | 68,523 |
|  | $1,069,082 | | | $1,075,252 |

Proceeds from maturities and sales of investment securities during 1990 were $416,358,000 resulting in gains of $489,000 and losses of $65,000.

•  •  •  •

J P MORGAN & CO. INCORPORATED, DECEMBER 31, 1990

*Notes to Financial Statements*

1.  Accounting policies

•  •  •  •

Debt securities held for investment

Debt securities classified as investment securities are held to meet longer-term investment objectives, including yield and liquidity management purposes. J.P. Morgan has the ability to hold such securities to maturity. These securities are carried at cost, adjusted for amortization of premiums and accretion of discounts, and are recorded as of their trade dates. If investment securities are identified as held for sale, they are carried at the lower of cost or market value. Gains and losses on dispositions of debt securities held for investment are generally computed by the specific identification method.

•  •  •  •

Trading account assets and securities sold, not yet purchased

Trading positions are taken to benefit from short-term movements in market prices and for market-making and distribution purposes....

•  •  •  •

5.  Investment securities

A comparison of the book and market values of investment securities at December 31, 1990, 1989, and 1988, follows. The market values of U.S. state and political subdivision securities are established with the assistance of independent pricing services and are based on available market data. Market prices often reflect transactions of relatively small size and are not necessarily indicative of the prices at which large amounts of particular issues could readily be sold or purchased.

|  | 1990 | | 1989 | | 1988 | |
|---|---|---|---|---|---|---|
| (*in millions*) | Book value | Market value | Book value | Market value | Book value | Market value |
| U.S. Treasury | $1,047 | $1,062 | $1,144 | $1,177 | $1,370 | $1,371 |

| (*in millions*) | 1990 Book Value | 1990 Market Value | 1989 Book Value | 1989 Market Value | 1988 Book Value | 1988 Market Value |
|---|---|---|---|---|---|---|
| U.S. government agency | 5,527 | 5,609 | 3,289 | 3,364 | 2,011 | 1,951 |
| U.S. state and political subdivision | 2,659 | 2,825 | 3,119 | 3,328 | 3,952 | 4,168 |
| U.S. corporate and bank debt | 911 | 902 | 1,094 | 1,090 | 1,607 | 1,586 |
| Foreign government (a) | 5,687 | 5,581 | 4,636 | 4,521 | 4,274 | 4,284 |
| Foreign corporate and bank debt | 2,619 | 2,576 | 2,524 | 2,503 | 2,456 | 2,463 |
| Other, including commercial paper | 91 | 94 | 488 | 490 | 627 | 626 |
| | $18,541 | $18,649 | $16,294 | $16,473 | $16,297 | $16,449 |

(a) Primarily includes debt of countries that are members of the Organization for Economic Cooperation and Development (OECD), composed of economically developed nations of Western Europe, North America, Asia, and the South Pacific.

A profile of the maturities of investment securities at December 31, 1990, follows:

| (*in millions*) | Within One Year | After One Year but Within Five | After Five Years but Within ten |
|---|---|---|---|
| U.S. Treasury | $ 133 | $ 466 | $ 130 |
| U.S. government agency (a) | 91 | 2,180 | 1,025 |
| U.S. state and political subdivision | 1 | 298 | 777 |
| U.S. corporate and bank debt (a) | 271 | 274 | 196 |
| Foreign government | 620 | 2,226 | 2,239 |
| Foreign corporate and bank debt (a) | 658 | 1,472 | 398 |
| Other, including commercial paper | 37 | — | — |
| Total investment securities | $1,811 | $6,916 | $4,765 |
| Market value | $1,790 | $6,889 | $4,750 |
| Net unrealized appreciation (depreciation) | $ (21) | $ (27) | $ (15) |

| | After ten Years but Within Twenty | After Twenty Years | Total |
|---|---|---|---|
| U.S. Treasury | $ 81 | $ 237 | $ 1,047 |
| U.S. government agency (a) | 2,205 | 26 | 5,527 |
| U.S. state and political subdivision | 1,100 | 483 | 2,659 |
| U.S. corporate and bank debt (a) | 129 | 41 | 911 |
| Foreign government | 301 | 301 | 5,687 |
| Foreign corporate and bank debt (a) | 20 | 71 | 2,619 |
| Other, including commercial paper | — | 54 | 91 |
| Total investment securities | $3,836 | $1,213 | $18,541 |
| Market value | $3,958 | $1,262 | $18,649 |
| Net unrealized appreciation (depreciation) | $ 122 | $ 49 | $ 108 |

(a) Mortgage-backed securities are included in the above table based primarily on their weighted-average maturities.

24

At December 31, 1990, gross unrealized appreciation and depreciation related to investment securities were as follows:

| (in millions) | Gross Unrealized Appreciation | Gross Unrealized Depreciation | Net Unrealized Appreciation (Depreciation) |
|---|---|---|---|
| U.S. Treasury | $ 18 | $ 3 | $ 15 |
| U.S. government agency | 94 | 12 | 82 |
| U.S. state and political subdivision | 196 | 30 | 166 |
| U.S. corporate and bank debt | 6 | 15 | (9) |
| Foreign government | 49 | 155 | (106) |
| Foreign corporate and bank debt | 14 | 57 | (43) |
| Other, including commercial paper | 6 | 3 | 3 |
| | $383 | $275 | $108 |

The following table presents gross realized gains and losses from dispositions of investment securities during 1990.

| (in millions) | 1990 |
|---|---|
| Gross realized gains from sales | $ 83 |
| Gross realized losses from sales | (72) |
| Net losses on maturities, calls, and mandatory redemptions | (9) |
| Net investment securities gains | 2 |

# SAVINGS INSTITUTIONS, FEDERALLY CHARTERED

H. F. AHMANSON & COMPANY, DECEMBER 31, 1990

*H.F. Ahmanson & Company and Subsidiaries*
*Notes to Consolidated Financial Statements*
*December 31, 1990, 1989 and 1988*

1. Summary of Significant Accounting Policies

• • • •

Cash, Cash Equivalents and Other Investment Securities

• • • •

Investments in debt securities are carried at amortized cost since management intends and has the ability to hold such securities until maturity or for the foreseeable future. Should an other than temporary decline in the value of a security in the portfolio occur, the carrying value of such security would be written down to current market value by a charge to operations.

Loans Receivable and MBSS

The Company periodically identifies loans and MBSS that are expected to be sold. Such loans and MBSS, which include most fixed rate loans originated subsequent to January 1, 1988, are carried at the lower of cost or market. It is the intent of the Company, and the Company has the ability, to hold all other loans and MBSS for the foreseeable future or until maturity. Accordingly, these other loans and MBSS are carried at cost, adjusted for unamortized discounts and loan fees.

The Company could sell loans and MBSS that were previously held for investment in response to unforeseeable circumstances. In the past, such circumstances have included unforeseen deposit outflows that would have caused a liquidity shortfall, changes in the availability and attractiveness of alternative sources of funds, excess loan demand by borrowers that could not be controlled immediately by loan pricing changes, restructure of the Company's recourse liability on MBSS, and changes in regulatory minimum capital requirements. Because sales of loans and MBSS held for investment are influenced by such unforeseeable circumstances, the level of future sales, if any, is difficult to predict. However, such sales are expected to be unusual and would not be expected to result in any material loss under current conditions.

• • • •

3. Investment Securities

• • • •

Other investment securities [*Ed. Note:* *Other than securities purchased under agreements to be resold*] are summarized as follows:

| (in thousands) | Book Value | Gross Unrealized Gains | Gross Unrealized Losses | Market Value |
|---|---|---|---|---|
| December 31, 1990 | | | | |
| United States Government and Federal Agency obligations | $125,257 | $ 938 | $ (456) | $125,739 |
| Public utility, industrial and other obligations | 95,508 | 21 | (6,307) | 89,222 |
| State, county and municipal obligations | 21,974 | 13 | (168) | 21,819 |
| | $276,336 | $ 972 | $(6,931) | $270,377 |
| December 31, 1989 | | | | |
| United States Government and Federal Agency obligations | $186,659 | $ 788 | $ (568) | $186,879 |
| Public utility, industrial and other obligations | 150,287 | 195 | (6,867) | 143,615 |
| State, county and municipal obligations | 22,878 | 28 | (77) | 22,829 |
| • • • • | | | | |
| | $407,945 | $1,011 | $(7,512) | $401,444 |

The contractual maturities of debt securities at December 31, 1990 are:

| (*in thousands*) | Amortized Cost | Market Value |
|---|---|---|
| One year or less | $ 81,844 | $ 82,009 |
| After one year through five years | 74,980 | 74,493 |
| After five years through ten years | 29,951 | 27,393 |
| After ten years | 55,964 | 52,885 |
| | $242,739 | $236,780 |

The following table represents proceeds from sales of debt securities and gross realized gains and losses on such sales for the periods indicated:

| (*in thousands*) | Years Ended December 31, | | |
|---|---|---|---|
| | 1990 | 1989 | 1988 |
| Proceeds from sales | $148,060 | $262,355 | $1,090,129 |
| Gross realized gains | $   2,113 | $   2,766 | $      999 |
| Gross realized losses | (4,249) | (256) | (28) |
| Net gains (losses) | $  (2,136) | $   2,510 | $      971 |

● ● ● ●

4.  Loans, MBSS and Mortgage Banking Activities

The loan and MBS portfolio ("loan portfolio") is summarized as follows:

| (*in thousands*) | December 31, | |
|---|---|---|
| | 1990 | 1989 |

● ● ● ●

| | | |
|---|---|---|
| Total loans receivable | 37,570,422 | 33,166,260 |
| MBSS, less unearned income of $5,380 (1990) and $478 (1989) | 5,113,597 | 5,539,381 |
| Loans and MBSS held for sale less unearned income of $5,771 (1990) and $5,231 (1989) | 2,154,991 | 960,093 |
| Total loans receivable and MBSS | $44,839,010 | $39,665,734 |

● ● ● ●

Loans and MBSS held for sale are summarized as follows:

| December 31, | 1990 | | 1989 | |
|---|---|---|---|---|
| (*in thousands*) | Amortized Cost | Market Value | Amortized Cost | Market Value |
| Adjustable rate MBSS | $2,117,917 | $2,152,400 | $822,949 | $843,854 |

● ● ● ●

| | $2,154,991 | $2,190,223 | $960,093 | $989,132 |
|---|---|---|---|---|

The MBSS owned by the Company, excluding MBSS held for sale, at December 31, 1990 and 1989, consisted of the following:

27

| (in thousands) | Amortized Cost | Gross Unrealized Gains | Gross Unrealized Losses | Market Value |
|---|---|---|---|---|
| **December 31, 1990** | | | | |
| FNMA | $3,852,340 | $55,682 | $(41,543) | $3,866,479 |
| GNMA | 157,841 | 482 | (5,968) | 152,355 |
| FHLMC | 1,103,416 | 19,273 | (1,726) | 1,120,963 |
| | $5,113,597 | $75,437 | $(49,237) | $5,139,797 |
| **December 31, 1989** | | | | |
| FNMA | $5,317,573 | $79,643 | $(50,852) | $5,346,364 |
| GNMA | 174,928 | 655 | (6,778) | 168,805 |
| FHLMC | 46,880 | 754 | (1,512) | 46,122 |
| | $5,539,381 | $81,052 | $(59,142) | $5,561,291 |

•  •  •  •

The following table represents proceeds from sales of MBSS and gross realized gains and losses on such sales for the periods indicated:

| (in thousands) | Years Ended December 31, | | |
|---|---|---|---|
| | 1990 | 1989 | 1988 |
| Proceeds from sales | $1,280,976 | $2,282,284 | $3,563,006 |
| Gross realized gains | $   15,151 | $   26,146 | $   50,020 |
| Gross realized losses | (64) | (448) | (544) |
| Net gains | $   15,087 | $   25,698 | $   49,476 |

•  •  •  •

CALFED INC., DECEMBER 31, 1990

*Notes to Consolidated Financial Statements*

Note 1:  Summary of Significant Accounting Policies

Principles of Consolidation

•  •  •  •

Investment Securities

Investment securities are carried at cost, adjusted for the amortization of the related discounts or the accretion of the related discounts into interest income using the level-yield method over the estimated remaining period until maturity.

•  •  •  •

Unrealized losses on securities which reflect a permanent decline in value are charged to income and reported under the caption "Gain (loss) on sales of investments, net" in the consolidated financial statements. Gains and losses on sales of investment securities are computed on a specific identification cost basis.

It is the Company's intent to hold to maturity its portfolio of investment securities at December 31, 1990 as part of its portfolio of long term interest earning assets. The Company's intent to hold securities for investment is based upon an evaluation of the probability of the occurrence of future events and how such events may impact the Company's desire to hold the investments to maturity. Should the actual occurrence of events anticipated by the Company differ, in a substantial measure from the Company's forecast, the Company's intent to hold investment securities to maturity may be reevaluated.

## Mortgage-Backed Securities

Mortgage-backed securities are recorded at cost, net of premiums and discounts. The Company's portfolio of mortgage-backed securities consists of pools of mortgage loans exchanged for mortgage-backed securities ("securitized loans"). Additionally, the Company has created mortgage-backed securities by aggregating pools of loans as collateral for mortgage pass-through securities. Mortgage-backed securities are carried at the Company's investment in the underlying pool of mortgage loans at the time of the exchange, adjusted for principal amortization and any premiums or discounts. Any related discount or premium is accreted into interest income using the level-yield method over the remaining contractual life of the securities, adjusted for actual prepayments. Gains and losses from the sales of mortgage-backed securities are computed on a specific identification cost basis. Except for those mortgage-backed securities designated as held for sale, it is the Company's intent to hold its portfolio of mortgage-backed securities at December 31, 1990 to maturity. The Company's intent to hold mortgage-backed securities is based upon factors similar to those previously discussed in "Investment Securities" and upon other factors.

## Assets Held for Sale

The Company has designated certain of its loans and mortgage-backed securities as being held for sale. In determining the level of assets held for sale, the Company considers the current and anticipated regulatory capital requirements of the Bank, liquidity requirements, asset size, the composition and interest rate sensitivity of its loan and mortgage-backed securities portfolios and other factors.

● ● ● ●

Assets held for sale are carried at the lower of aggregate cost or market value by loan type and are included under the caption "Assets held for sale" in the consolidated statements of financial condition..... Gains or losses from the sale of mortgage-backed securities held for sale are included under the caption "Gain on sales of mortgage-backed securities, net" in the consolidated financial statements.

● ● ● ●

## Note 3: Investment Securities

Shown below are the carrying values and market values of investment securities at December 31, 1990 and 1989 with related maturity data:

| (dollars in millions) | 1990 | | 1989 | |
| --- | --- | --- | --- | --- |
| | Carrying Value | Market Value | Carrying Value | Market Value |
| U.S. Treasury securities: | | | | |
| Maturing within 1 year | $ .6 | $ .7 | $ .7 | $ .7 |
| Maturing after 1 year but within 5 years | — | — | — | — |

*Investment Securities (continued)*

| (dollars in millions) | 1990 | | 1989 | |
|---|---|---|---|---|
| | Carrying Value | Market Value | Carrying Value | Market Value |
| Maturing after 5 years but within 10 years | 1,026.3 | 994.6 | 1,026.5 | 983.3 |
| Maturing after 10 years | 81.2 | 80.2 | 81.2 | 82.8 |
| | 1,081.1 | 1,075.5 | 1,108.4 | 1,066.8 |
| Other U.S. Government entities: | | | | |
| Maturing within 1 year | 2.7 | 2.7 | 47.5 | 47.5 |
| Maturing after 1 year but within 5 years | — | — | 2.6 | 2.6 |
| Maturing after 5 years but within 10 years | 14.0 | 13.3 | 14.0 | 13.2 |
| Maturing after 10 years | — | — | 1.0 | 1.2 |
| | 16.7 | 16.0 | 65.1 | 64.5 |
| Other bonds, notes and debentures: | | | | |
| Maturing within 1 year | 1.6 | 1.5 | 27.8 | 27.8 |
| Maturing after 1 year but within 5 years | 11.1 | 11.1 | — | — |
| Maturing after 5 years but within 10 years | — | — | — | — |
| Maturing after 10 years | 2.6 | 2.7 | 2.0 | 2.1 |
| | 15.3 | 15.3 | 29.8 | 29.9 |
| FHLB Stock | 178.4 | 178.4 | 209.3 | 209.3 |
| Other investment securities | 10.6 | 10.6 | 6.8 | 6.3 |
| | 189.0 | 189.0 | 216.1 | 215.6 |
| | $1,329.1 | $1,295.8 | $1,419.4 | $1,376.8 |

.... The Company's portfolio of investment securities had gross unrealized losses of $33.3 million at December 31, 1990.

•••

The Company does not believe that any of its investment securities have suffered permanent impairment of value and the Company has the ability and intends to hold these securities to maturity.

Note 4: Mortgage-Backed Securities, Net

Summarized below are the carrying values and market values of mortgage-backed securities at December 31, 1990 and 1989:

| (dollars in millions) | 1990 | | 1989 | |
|---|---|---|---|---|
| | Carrying Value | Market Value | Carrying Value | Market Value |
| FNMA | $1,008.3 | $1,028.7 | $1,528.9 | $1,554.5 |
| California Federal AA-rated mortgage pass-through securities | 450.8 | 459.5 | 88.9 | 89.2 |
| Other | 98.5 | 65.0 | 213.4 | 198.8 |
| | $1,557.6 | $1,553.2 | $1,831.2 | $1,842.5 |

The entire portfolio of the Company's mortgage-backed securities at December 31, 1990 had contractual maturities in excess of ten years. The Company's mortgage-backed securities had gross unrealized losses of $4.4 million at December 31, 1990.

••••

Note 6:  Assets Held for Sale

In order to manage its asset size, liquidity requirements, composition and interest rate sensitivity of its interest-earning assets and other factors, the Company holds certain assets for sale. The table below presents such assets and their respective market values at December 31, 1990 and 1989:

| (*dollars in millions*) | 1990 | | 1989 | |
| --- | --- | --- | --- | --- |
| | Cost Basis | Market Value | Cost Basis | Market Value |
| ••••  | | | | |
| Mortgage-backed securities | 1,049.0 | 1,050.0 | — | — |
| | $1,618.1 | $1,619.2 | $744.5 | $753.0 |

The amounts presented above at December 31, 1990 are net of a lower of cost or market allowance of $9.4 million for unrealized losses. There was no such allowance at December 31, 1989.  At December 31, 1990, gross unrealized gains on assets held for sale totaled $1.1 million.

CHARTER ONE FINANCIAL INC., DECEMBER 31, 1990

*Notes to Consolidated Financial Statements*

1.   Summary of Significant Accounting Policies

••••

Investment Securities

The Company generally acquires investment securities with the intent to hold them until maturity.  Investment securities held for investment are carried at cost and are adjusted for amortization of premiums and accretion of discounts over the lives of the securities.... Gains or losses on sale of investment securities are recorded based on the adjusted cost of the specific securities sold.

••••

Loans and Mortgage-Backed Securities

The Company originates loans and acquires mortgage-backed securities primarily for portfolio investment.  Loans and mortgage-backed securities held for investment are stated at the principal amount outstanding adjusted for amortization of premiums and accretion of discounts using the interest method.  Interest is accrued as earned.

••••

Classification of Financial Instruments

Sales of investment securities, loans and mortgage-backed securities are dependent upon various factors, including interest rate movements, deposit flows, the availability and attractiveness of other sources of funds, loan demand by borrowers and liquidity and capital requirements. Due to the volatility and unpredictability of these factors, investment securities, loans and mortgage-backed securities may be sold prior to maturity. The Company re-evaluates its intent to hold these financial instruments at each balance sheet date for the ensuing year based on the then current environment and, if appropriate, reclassifies them as held for sale. Financial instruments held for sale are carried at the lower of cost or market.

•••• 

3. Investment Securities

Investment securities consist of the following:

| (in thousands) | Carrying Value | Market Value | Gross Unrealized Gains | Gross Unrealized Losses |
|---|---|---|---|---|
| December 31, 1990 | | | | |
| Held for investment: | | | | |
| U.S. Government and Federal agency obligations | $168,958 | $170,251 | $1,780 | $ 487 |
| Floating rate notes, commercial paper and other | 60,081 | 59,249 | 88 | 920 |
| State and local government obligations | 377 | 379 | 3 | 1 |
| Total | $229,416 | $229,879 | $1,871 | $1,408 |

•••• 

| (in thousands) | Carrying Value | Market Value | Gross Unrealized Gains | Gross Unrealized Losses |
|---|---|---|---|---|
| December 31, 1989 | | | | |
| Held for investment: | | | | |
| U.S. Government and Federal agency obligations | $ 38,751 | $ 38,547 | $    81 | $ 285 |
| Floating rate notes and commercial paper | 74,588 | 74,602 | 103 | 89 |
| Bankers' acceptances | 1,993 | 2,000 | 7 | — |
| State and local government obligations | 417 | 417 | — | — |
| Marketable equity securities | 16,840 | 31,088 | 14,843 | $ 595 |
| Total | $132,589 | $146,654 | $15,034 | $ 969 |

•••• 

Substantially all of the Company's portfolio of floating rate notes and commercial paper were issued by companies in the financial services industry and have investment grade ratings.

At December 31, 1990 and 1989, neither a disposal, nor conditions that could lead to a decision not to hold the debt securities classified as held for investment to maturity were reasonably foreseen.

A summary of debt securities by maturity follows:

32

| (dollars in thousands) | December 31, 1990 | | |
| --- | --- | --- | --- |
| | Book Value | Yield | Market Value |
| Due in one year or less | $125,624 | 9.25% | $125,541 |
| Due after one year through five years | 85,696 | 8.13 | 86,603 |
| Due after five years through ten years | 8,848 | 8.62 | 8,452 |
| Due after ten years | 9,248 | 8.79 | 9,283 |
| Total | $229,416 | 8.79 | $229,879 |

A summary of gross realized gains and gross realized losses on sales of investment securities follows:

| (in thousands) | For the Year Ended December 31, | Gross Realized Gains | Gross Realized Loss | Net Realized Gain |
| --- | --- | --- | --- | --- |
| | 1990 | $13,462 | $ 18 | $13,444 |
| | 1989 | 6,841 | 16 | 6,825 |
| | 1988 | 4,588 | 169 | 4,419 |

• • • •

4. Mortgage-Backed Securities

Mortgage-backed securities consist of the following:

| (in thousands) | December 31, | |
| --- | --- | --- |
| | 1990 | 1989 |
| Held for investment: | | |
| Participation certificates: | | |
| Federal Home Loan Mortgage Corporation | $136,516 | $ 56,646 |
| Federal National Mortgage Association | 33,045 | 16,481 |
| Government National Mortgage Association | 27,053 | 2,989 |
| Private issues | 133,836 | 65,134 |
| Collateralized mortgage obligations | 149,392 | 85,446 |
| Total | 479,842 | 226,696 |
| Less unamortized discounts—net | 10,525 | 4,282 |
| Total | 469,317 | 222,414 |
| Gross unrealized gains | 6,906 | 1,832 |
| Gross unrealized losses | (4,017) | (3,371) |
| Market value | $472,206 | $220,875 |
| Participation certificates held for sale | $125,263 | $ 6,879 |
| Market value | $128,272 | $ 6,956 |

• • • •

At December 31, 1990 and 1989, neither a disposal, nor conditions that could lead to a decision not to hold mortgage-backed securities classified as held for investment to maturity were reasonably foreseen.

CITIZENS SAVINGS FINANCIAL CORPORATION, DECEMBER 31, 1990

*Notes to Consolidated Financial Statements*
*Citizens Savings Financial Corporation and Subsidiaries*

1. Summary of Significant Accounting Policies

•••

Basis of Financial Statement Presentation

The Consolidated Financial Statements include the accounts of the Company and its subsidiaries, including Citizens Federal Bank, a Federal Savings Bank ("Citizens Federal"), and its subsidiaries, as applicable....

•••

Investments in Debt Securities

The Company's investment in securities consists of investment securities (corporate, municipal, agency, government and equity securities) and mortgage-backed securities. Debt securities held for investment are carried at cost (adjusted for amortization of premiums and discounts). Debt securities held for sale are stated at the lower of aggregate cost or market value. Net unrealized losses in the market value of debt securities held for sale are recorded as a reduction of income in the period in which they occur. Investment securities are primarily held by Citizens Federal for the purpose of meeting its minimum regulatory liquidity requirements. In this regard, additions to Citizens Federal's investment security portfolio are generally made in shorter term investments and with the intent to hold the investments in its portfolio in order to assist in meeting its minimum liquidity requirements. Primarily as a result of an increase in the level of prepayments due to lower interest rates and a higher volume of refinancings, and also in certain cases because of the decreasing creditworthiness of the issuers and/or the underlying collateral, the Company has approximately $51,002,000 of unhedged Aa-rated pass-through securities held for sale at December 31, 1990. Gain or loss on sale of investments is based on the specific identification method....

2. Investment Securities

A comparison of the book values and approximate market values of investment securities is as follows:

|  | Book Value | Gross Unrealized Gains | Gross Unrealized Losses | Market Value |
|---|---|---|---|---|
|  |  | *(in thousands)* | | |
| December 31, 1989 |  |  |  |  |
| Investment securities (1): |  |  |  |  |
| Due within 1 year: |  |  |  |  |
| Corporate notes (2) | $ 16,913 | $ 2 | $ (12) | $ 16,903 |
| Municipal bonds | 1,003 | — | (12) | 991 |
| U.S. agency notes | — | — | — | — |
| U.S. Treasury securities | 10,029 | — | — | 10,029 |
|  | 27,945 | 2 | (24) | 27,923 |

|  | Book Value | Gross Unrealized Gains | Gross Unrealized Losses | Market Value |
|---|---|---|---|---|
|  |  |  | (in thousands) |  |
| **Due after 1 through 5 years:** |  |  |  |  |
| Corporate notes (2)(3) | 16,920 | 68 | (68) | 16,920 |
| U.S. agency notes | — | — | — | — |
| FSLIC note (4) | — | — | — | — |
|  | 16,920 | 68 | (68) | 16,920 |
| **Due after 5 years through 10 years:** |  |  |  |  |
| U.S. agency notes | 1,420 | 89 | — | 1,509 |
| FSLIC note (4) | 25,000 | — | — | 25,000 |
|  | 26,420 | 89 | — | 26,509 |
| **Due after 10 years:** |  |  |  |  |
| Corporate notes (2) | 496 | — | (28) | 468 |
| U.S. agency notes | 823 | — | (46) | 777 |
|  | 1,319 | — | (74) | 1,245 |

•  •  •  •

|  | Book Value | Gross Unrealized Gains | Gross Unrealized Losses | Market Value |
|---|---|---|---|---|
|  | $ 153,767 | $ 159 | $ (166) | $153,760 |

### December 31, 1990

| Investment securities (1): | Book Value | Gross Unrealized Gains | Gross Unrealized Losses | Market Value |
|---|---|---|---|---|
| **Due within 1 year:** |  |  |  |  |
| Corporate notes (2) | $ 3,998 | $ 39 | $ — | $ 4,037 |
| Municipal bonds | — | — | — | — |
| U.S. agency notes | 1,993 | 31 | — | 2,024 |
| U.S. Treasury securities | — | — | — | — |
|  | 5,991 | 70 | — | 6,061 |
| **Due after 1 through 5 years:** |  |  |  |  |
| Corporate notes (2)(3) | 7,921 | 99 | — | 8,020 |
| U.S. agency notes | 5,857 | 98 | — | 5,955 |
| FSLIC note (4) | 25,000 | — | — | 25,000 |
|  | 38,778 | 197 | — | 38,975 |
| **Due after 5 years through 10 years:** |  |  |  |  |
| U.S. agency notes | 1,445 | 82 | — | 1,527 |
| FSLIC note (4) | — | — | — | — |
|  | 1,445 | 82 | — | 1,527 |
| **Due after 10 years:** |  |  |  |  |
| Corporate notes (2) | — | — | — | — |
| U.S. agency notes | 807 | — | (15) | 792 |
|  | 807 | — | (15) | 792 |

•  •  •  •

|  | Book Value | Gross Unrealized Gains | Gross Unrealized Losses | Market Value |
|---|---|---|---|---|
|  | $110,175 | $ 349 | $ (15) | $110,509 |

(1) Proceeds from sales of investment securities and gross realized gains and losses on those sales during the years ended December 31, 1988, 1989 and 1990 are as follows:

|  | Year Ended December 31, | | |
|  | 1988 | 1989 | 1990 |
|  | *(in thousands)* | | |
| Sales proceeds: | | | |
| Investment securities | $61,409 | $51,353 | $25,878 |
| Equity securities | $ 7,153 | $34,309 | $ 2,971 |
| Realized gains: | | | |
| Investment securities | $   801 | $ 1,782 | $     15 |
| Equity securities | $   966 | $ 1,961 | $   348 |
| Realized losses: | | | |
| Investment securities | $   416 | $     20 | $     84 |
| Equity securities | $   641 | $   599 | $   181 |

(2) All corporate notes are of investment grade.

(3) At December 31, 1990 Citizens Federal has pledged approximately $1,933,000 in corporate notes as collateral for certain subserviced loans.

(4) On March 6, 1991 the FSLIC note was prepaid in full (see Note 20 to the Consolidated Financial Statements). [*Ed. Note: Note 20 is omitted from this survey*]

•••

4.  Mortgage-Backed Securities

Summarized below are the book values and approximate market values of mortgage-backed securities:

|  | Book Value | Gross Unrealized Gains | Gross Unrealized Losses | Market Value |
|  | *(in thousands)* | | | |
| **December 31, 1989** | | | | |
| FNMA | $    54,839 | $   1,103 | $     (936) | $     55,006 |
| FHLMC | 187,681 | 3,067 | (3,279) | 187,469 |
| FNMA | 79,759 | 588 | (3,384) | 76,963 |
| Collateralized mortgage obligations | 198,756 | 10,095 | (4,038) | 204,813 |
| Rated non-agency pass-through securities | 668,653 | 3,040 | (10,223) | 661,470 |
|  | $1,189,688 | $17,893 | $(21,860) | $1,185,721 |
| **December 31, 1990** | | | | |
| GNMA | $    24,587 | $      214 | $     (805) | $     23,996 |
| FHLMC | 110,081 | 290 | (3,211) | 107,160 |
| FNMA | 41,358 | 242 | (3,092) | 38,508 |
| Collateralized mortgage obligations | 294,807 | 7,324 | (2,913) | 299,218 |
| Rated non-agency pass-through securities | 627,578 | 1,774 | (9,267) | 620,085 |
|  | $1,098,411 | $ 9,844 | $(19,288) | $1,088,967 |

36

••••

Rated non-agency pass-through securities with a book value of $51,002,000 and a market value of $52,091,000 are held for sale at December 31, 1990.

••••

Proceeds from sales of mortgage-backed securities and gross realized gains and losses on those sales during the years ended December 31, 1988, 1989 and 1990 are as follows:

|  | Year Ended December 31, | | |
| --- | --- | --- | --- |
|  | 1988 | 1989 | 1990 |
|  | (*in thousands*) | | |
| Sales proceeds | $290,529 | $121,497 | $208,252 |
| Realized gains | $ 10,592 | $ 8,521 | $ 5,245 |
| Realized losses | $ — | $ — | $ 42 |

HOMEFED CORPORATION, DECEMBER 31, 1990

*Homefed Corporation and Subsidiaries*
*Notes to Consolidated Financial Statements*

1.  Summary of Significant Accounting Policies

••••

C.  Marketable Securities

Marketable securities held for investment are carried at cost, adjusted for amortization of premium and accretion of discount over the term of the security. These investments are not carried at the lower of cost or market, in that management has both the intent and ability to hold them for the foreseeable future or until maturity. Certain marketable securities are held for sale and are carried at the lower of amortized cost or market value. See Note 2 to the Consolidated Financial Statements.

••••

G.  Gain on Sale of Loans and Securities

The Company has sold whole loans, mortgage loan participations, mortgage-backed securities ("MBSs") and various other securities. Certain loans and securities are held for sale and are carried at the lower of cost or market (see notes 2, 3, 4, 5 and 24 to the Consolidated Financial Statements). [**Ed. Note:** *Notes 3, 5, and 24 are omitted from this survey.*] The remaining loans and securities are carried at cost as management has both the intent and ability to hold such loans and securities for the foreseeable future or until maturity. The Company may sell loans and securities that are held as investments under certain unforeseen circumstances such as unanticipated deposit outflows which would create a liquidity shortfall, unexpected changes in the availability and terms of other sources of funds or unforeseen changes in regulatory capital requirements. Because of such unforeseen events, the level of future sales of loans and securities held for investment is difficult to predict. When sales of loans and securities do occur, a gain or loss is recognized to the extent that the sales proceeds exceed or are less than the book value (net of unearned discount or premium at date of sale) of the loans and securities. In certain instances, the Company receives cash proceeds equal to the principal amount of loans sold but with yield rates which reflect the current market rate. The premium or discount is adjusted periodically for loan prepayments in excess of estimated prepayments....

• • • •

2. Marketable Securities and Other Short-Term Investments

Marketable securities and other short-term investments at December 31 are summarized as follows:

| (*dollar amounts in thousands*) | 1990 | | | |
| --- | --- | --- | --- | --- |
| | Book Value | Gross Unrealized Gains | Gross Unrealized Losses | Estimated Market Value |
| Repurchase agreements | $ 15,917 | $ — | $ — | $ 15,917 |
| Certificates of deposit | 10,604 | 10 | — | 10,614 |
| Corporate debt securities | 28,408 | — | (67) | 28,341 |
| U.S. government and federal agency securities | 576,032 | 1,075 | (24) | 577,083 |
| Term federal funds | 20,000 | — | — | 20,000 |
| Commercial paper | -- | — | — | — |
| | $650,961 | $1,085 | $ (91) | $651,955 |

| | 1989 | |
| --- | --- | --- |
| | Book Value | Estimated Market Value |
| Repurchase agreements | $ 25,000 | $ 25,000 |
| Certificates of deposit | 155,694 | 155,818 |
| Corporate debt securities | 31,374 | 31,373 |
| U.S. government and federal agency securities | 30,925 | 31,125 |
| Term federal funds | 50,000 | 50,000 |
| Commercial paper | 19,994 | 19,778 |
| | $312,987 | $313,094 |

The weighted average interest rates of marketable securities and other short-term investments at December 31, 1990 and 1989 were 6.96% and 8.23%, respectively.

• • • •

The Company had marketable securities and other short-term investments held for sale, recorded at the lower of amortized cost or market value as of December 31, 1990 and 1989 in the amount of $575,667,000 and $10,100,000, respectively.

The amortized cost and estimated market value of marketable securities at December 31, 1990, by contractual maturity are shown below. Actual maturities may differ from contractual maturities because issuers may have the right to call or prepay obligations with or without call or prepayment penalties.

38

| *(dollars amounts in thousands)* | | |
|---|---|---|
| | | Estimated |
| | Book | Market |
| Period | Value | Value |
| 1991 | $543,669 | $543,794 |
| 1992-1995 | 94,003 | 94,827 |
| 1996-2000 | 13,289 | 13,334 |
| | $650,961 | $651,955 |

Proceeds from the sales of marketable securities were $1,368,854,000 for the year ended December 31, 1990. Gross gains of $1,117,000 and gross losses of $1,868,000 were realized in connection with those sales.

4. Mortgage-Backed Securities

Mortgage-backed securities at December 31 are summarized as follows:

*(dollar amounts in thousands)*

| | 1990 | | | |
|---|---|---|---|---|
| | | Gross | Gross | Estimated |
| | Book | Unrealized | Unrealized | Market |
| | Value | Gains | Losses | Value |
| FNMA | $ 384,732 | $1,563 | ($11,893) | $ 374,402 |
| FHLMC | 240,347 | 255 | (3,249) | 237,353 |
| GNMA | 335,177 | 6,969 | — | 342,146 |
| CMO (1) | 22,028 | — | — | 22,028 |
| Other (2) | 79,442 | — | (10,615) | 68,827 |
| | $1,061,726 | $8,787 | ($25,757) | $1,044,756 |

| | 1989 | |
|---|---|---|
| | | Estimated |
| | Book | Market |
| | Value | Value |
| FNMA | $583,710 | $561,210 |
| FHLMC | 279,577 | 270,735 |
| GNMA | 25,110 | 25,061 |
| CMO (1) | 18,996 | 18,996 |
| Other (2) | 79,540 | 69,597 |
| | $986,933 | $945,599 |

(1) Represents bonds collateralized by FNMA and FHLMC mortgage-backed securities collateralized by whole loans.

(2) Represents mortgage-backed securities which are a fully subordinated interest in loans sold totaling approximately $524,393,000.

• • • •

Included in mortgage-backed securities are securities held for sale, recorded at the lower of amortized cost or market value, at December 31, 1990 and 1989 in the amount of $32,732,000 and $116,880,000, respectively.

Substantially all mortgage-backed securities are pass-through securities and as such, have no stated contractual maturity.

Proceeds from the sales of mortgage-backed securities were $1,018,605,000 for the year ended

December 31, 1990.  Gross gains of $9,601,000 and gross losses of $2,145,000 were realized in connection with these sales.

•••• 

METROPOLITAN FINANCIAL CORPORATION, DECEMBER 31, 1990

*Notes to Consolidated Financial Statements*

Note A—Summary of Significant Accounting Policies

•••• 

Investments and Mortgage-Backed Securities

Investments and mortgage-backed securities held for investment are stated at cost, adjusted for amortization of premiums and accretion of discounts.  The carrying value of investments and mortgage-backed securities is adjusted to the lower of cost or market when permanent declines in value occur or when management has elected to sell individual securities.  Gain or loss on sale of securities is based on the specific identification method.

•••• 

Note C—Investment Securities

Investment securities consisted of the following (*in thousands*):

|  | Book Value | Gross Unrealized Gains | Gross Unrealized Losses | Estimated Market Value |
|---|---|---|---|---|
| December 31, 1990 |  |  |  |  |
| United States Treasury | $ 65,688 | $ 151 | $(3,497) | $ 62,342 |
| United States government agencies | 67,573 | 1,781 | (3) | 69,351 |
| Corporate debt securities | 67,569 | 117 | — | 67,686 |
| Other | 3,447 | — | — | 3,447 |
|  | $204,277 | $2,049 | $(3,500) | $202,826 |
| December 31, 1989 |  |  |  |  |
| United States Treasury | $ 81,053 | $ 346 | $(2,603) | $ 78,796 |
| United States government agencies | 31,971 | 349 | — | 32,320 |
| Corporate debt securities | 32,469 | 191 | (12) | 32,648 |
| Other | 26,671 | 1 | — | 26,672 |
|  | $172,164 | $ 887 | $(2,615) | $170,436 |

The book value and market value of investment securities by contractual maturity at December 31, 1990, are as follows:

|  | Book Value | Market Value |
|---|---|---|
| One year or less | $ 73,782 | $ 73,815 |
| One year through five years | 88,415 | 90,428 |
| Five years through ten years | 346 | 346 |

|  | Book Value | Market Value |
|---|---|---|
| Ten years and after | 41,734 | 38,237 |
|  | $204,277 | $202,826 |

Proceeds from sales of investment securities were $162,877,000, $98,669,000 and $168,095,000 during 1990, 1989 and 1988, respectively. Gross gains of $232,000, $659,000 and $1,920,000 were realized in 1990, 1989 and 1988.

•••• 

## Note D—Mortgage Backed Securities

Mortgage backed securities consisted of the following (*in thousands*):

| | December 31 | | | |
|---|---|---|---|---|
| | 1990 | | 1989 | |
| | Book Value | Market Value | Book Value | Market Value |
| GNMA | $ 994,150 | $1,001,649 | $ 608,235 | $ 602,893 |
| FNMA | 91,786 | 90,194 | 144,776 | 143,976 |
| FHLMC | 275,806 | 274,147 | 257,352 | 254,546 |
| Other | 149,714 | 149,672 | 47,332 | 46,074 |
| | $1,511,456 | $1,515,662 | $1,057,695 | $1,047,489 |

Proceeds from the sale of mortgage-backed securities were $163,521,000, $283,663,000 and $31,646,000 during 1990, 1989 and 1988, respectively. Gross gains of $2,906,000, $7,287,000 and $829,000, and gross losses of $71,000, $2,658,000 and $53,000 were realized on those sales.

The market value of mortgage backed securities consists of gross unrealized gains of $21,533,000 and $11,813,000 and gross unrealized losses of $17,327,000 and $22,019,000 for 1990 and 1989, respectively.

•••• 

At December 31, 1990, $104 million of mortgage-backed securities had been sold with January 1991 settlement dates and $59 million of securities at December 31, 1989, had been sold with a January 1990 settlement date. Such securities are included in mortgage-backed securities at the respective year end.

## SAVINGS INSTITUTIONS, STATE CHARTERED

AMERICAN BANK OF CONNECTICUT, DECEMBER 31, 1990

*Notes to Financial Statements*

Summary of Accounting Policies

•••• 

(c) Investment Securities

Investment securities with fixed maturities are carried at amortized cost. Such securities are not carried at the lower of cost or market as management intends to hold the securities for the foreseeable future....

••••

Gains and losses on sales of investment securities are determined on the specific identification method and are recognized upon realization.

••••

Investment Securities

A comparative summary follows (*in thousands*):

| | Principal Amount | Amortized Cost | Quoted Market Value |
|---|---|---|---|
| **December 31, 1990** | | | |
| | | | |
| Fixed-term securities: | | | |
| U.S. Government and agency obligations maturing within: | | | |
| One year | $1,000 | $ 1,000 | $ 1,011 |
| One to five years | 2,000 | 2,002 | 2,028 |
| | 3,000 | 3,002 | 3,039 |
| Tax-exempt bonds maturing within: | | | |
| One to five years | 2,070 | 2,118 | 2,136 |
| Six to ten years | 250 | 250 | 250 |
| Over ten years | 2,500 | 2,482 | 2,401 |
| | $7,820 | $ 7,852 | $ 7,826 |
| Preferred stock | | $12,555 | $12,430 |

••••

| | | $42,592 | $42,566 |
|---|---|---|---|
| **December 31, 1989** | | | |
| | | | |
| Fixed-term securities: | | | |
| U.S. Government and agency obligations maturing within: | | | |
| One year | $3,047 | $ 3,048 | $ 3,045 |
| One to five years | 3,000 | 3,002 | 3,012 |
| | 6,047 | 6,050 | 6,057 |
| Tax-exempt bonds maturing within: | | | |
| One to five years | 0 | 0 | 0 |
| Six to ten years | 250 | 250 | 260 |
| Over ten years | 2,750 | 2,731 | 2,647 |
| | $9,047 | $ 9,031 | $ 8,964 |
| Preferred stock | | $ 8,891 | $ 9,931 |

••••

| | | $56,507 | $65,437 |
|---|---|---|---|

Amortized cost, gross unrealized gains and losses and estimated market values of debt securities are as follows at December 31, 1990 (*in thousands*):

|  | Amortized Cost | Gross Unrealized Gains | Gross Unrealized Losses | Estimated Market Value |
|---|---|---|---|---|
| U.S. Treasury securities and obligations of U.S. Government and agencies | $ 3,002 | $37 | $ 0 | $ 3,039 |
| Obligations of states and political subdivisions | 4,850 | 22 | (85) | 4,787 |
| Debt securities issued by foreign governments | 35 | 0 | 0 | 35 |
| Other debt securities | 7,328 | 14 | (44) | 7,298 |
| Totals | $15,215 | $73 | $(129) | $15,159 |

Other debt securities include preferred stock that, by its term, either must be redeemed by the issuing enterprise or is redeemable at the option of the investor.

The amortized cost and estimated market value of debt securities at December 31, 1990, by contractual maturity are shown below (*in thousands*). Expected maturities will differ from contractual maturities because borrowers may have the right to call or prepay obligations with or without call or prepayment penalties.

|  | Amortized Cost | Estimated Market Value |
|---|---|---|
| Due in one year or less | $ 5,000 | $ 5,011 |
| Due after one year through five years | 4,197 | 4,239 |
| Due after five years through ten years | 1,084 | 1,079 |
| Due after ten years | 4,934 | 4,830 |
|  | $15,215 | $15,159 |

Gains from sales of investments in debt securities during 1990 were approximately $64,000. Gross gains of $66,000 and gross losses of $2,000 were realized on those sales.

FIRST REPUBLIC BANCORP INC., DECEMBER 31, 1990

*Notes to Consolidated Financial Statements*

1. Summary of significant accounting policies

••••

Investment securities

Investment securities are accounted for according to their purpose. Securities acquired for investment purposes, including debt securities acquired with intent to hold for the foreseeable future, are recorded at historical cost, adjusted for amortization of premium and accretion of discount, where appropriate. If the Company should become unable to hold a debt security to maturity it is recorded at the lower of cost or market value. Declines in value that are considered other than temporary are recorded as losses on investment securities. Realized gains and losses on the sale of investment securities are computed based on the cost basis of securities specifically indentified.

• • • •

3. Investment Securities

The following summarizes by category the carrying value and approximate market value of investment securities at December 31:

|  | Carrying Value | Market Value |
|---|---|---|
| **1989** | | |
| U.S. Government and Agency | $21,376,000 | $21,382,000 |
| Mortgage-Backed Securities | 29,428,000 | 29,573,000 |
| Corporate Bonds and Other | 5,403,000 | 4,670,000 |
| Fixed-Income Fund Securities | 4,522,000 | 4,522,000 |
|  | $60,729,000 | $60,147,000 |
| **1990** | | |
| U.S. Government and Agency | $51,210,000 | $51,336,000 |
| Mortgage-Backed Securities | 11,843,000 | 11,747,000 |
| Corporate Bonds and Other | 5,509,000 | 4,987,000 |
| Fixed-Income Fund Securities | 3,287,000 | 3,287,000 |
|  | $71,849,000 | $71,357,000 |

At December 31, 1990, approximately $68,037,000, or 95%, of investment securities carried interest rates which adjust annually or more frequently.

• • • •

DIME SAVINGS BANK OF NEW YORK, DECEMBER 31, 1990

*Notes to Consolidated Financial Statements*

Note 1—Summary of Significant Accounting Policies

• • • •

(c) Investment Securities

Because the Bank has the ability to hold investment securities to maturity and the intent to hold them for the foreseeable future, bonds, notes and other securities are held for investment and are carried at cost less an allowance for losses, adjusted for amortization of premium and accretion of discount using the level yield method. Premiums are amortized to maturity or call date, while discounts are accreted to maturity.

• • • •

Gains and losses on the sale of investment securities are determined using the specific identification method.

• • • •

(d) Loans

.... Government National Mortgage Association ("GNMA"), Federal National Mortgage Association ("FNMA"), and Federal Home Loan Mortgage Corporation ("FHLMC") mortgage-backed certificates held for investment are carried at cost, adjusted for amortization of premium and accretion of discount using the level yield method over the estimated average life of the certificates. The Bank has the ability to hold the certificates to maturity and the intent to hold them for the foreseeable future.

• • • •

Loans and mortgage-backed certificates held for sale are carried at the lower of cost or estimated market value, determined on an aggregate basis.

• • • •

In response to previously-unforeseen events, such as changes in regulatory capital requirements, liquidity shortfalls or adverse changes in the availability of sources of funds, the Bank may sell loans, mortgage-backed certificates and investment securities which previously had been held for investment purposes. The impact of future sales of such assets, if any, cannot be predicted with certainty.

• • • •

(f) Allowances for Losses

The Bank uses the reserve method of accounting for credit losses, including losses on loans and investment securities....

The balance in the allowance for investment securities losses is determined based on management's review and evaluation of the investment securities portfolio to determine the existence of any permanent impairment. The allowance is then adjusted by a charging or crediting to expense. Recognized losses on such securities are charged to the allowance.

• • • •

Note 2—Investment Securities

The book values and estimated market values of investment securities are as follows:

| | December 31, 1990 | | December 31, 1989 | |
| --- | --- | --- | --- | --- |
| | Book Value | Estimated Market Value | Book Value | Estimated Market Value |
| | *(in thousands)* | | | |
| United States Government and Federal agencies | $ 64,171 | $ 64,455 | $183,816 | $182,153 |
| Other Investment Securities: | | | | |
| Other Bonds: | | | | |
| State and municipal obligations | 284,283 | 263,600 | 288,965 | 260,606 |
| Corporate and other obligations | 106,143 | 89,555 | 112,581 | 95,163 |
| Total other bonds | 390,426 | 353,155 | 401,546 | 355,769 |
| Less allowance for losses | 1,259 | — | 1,294 | — |
| Total other bonds, net | 389,167 | 353,155 | 400,252 | 355,769 |
| • • • • | | | | |
| Total other investment securities, net | $447,390 | $406,620 | $457,601 | $408,775 |

• • • •

Gross unrealized gains and losses for United States Government and Federal agencies, and other bonds as of December 31, 1990 are as follows:

| | Gross Gains | Unrealized Losses | Net Unrealized Gains (Losses) |
| --- | --- | --- | --- |
| | | *(in thousands)* | |
| United States Government and Federal agencies | $ 972 | ($ 688) | $ 284 |
| State and municipal obligations | 475 | (21,158) | ($20,683) |
| Corporate and other obligations | — | (16,588) | ($16,588) |
| Total unrealized gains and losses | $1,447 | ($38,434) | ($36,987) |

The book values and estimated market values for United States Government and Federal agencies, and other bonds at December 31, 1990 by contractual maturity are shown below. Expected maturities will differ from contractual maturities because certain issues are callable with or without call premiums.

| | Book Value | Estimated Market Value |
| --- | --- | --- |
| | *(in thousands)* | |
| Due in one year or less | $ 1,640 | $ 1,623 |
| Due after one year through five years | 68,026 | 67,818 |
| Due after five years through ten years | 50,785 | 46,454 |
| Due after ten years | 334,146 | 301,715 |
| Total United States Government and Federal agencies, and other bonds | $454,597 | $417,610 |

46

••••

Proceeds from sales of United States Government and Federal agencies, and other bonds along with related gross gains and losses for the periods indicated follows:

|  | For the years ended December 31, | | |
| --- | --- | --- | --- |
|  | 1990 | 1989 | 1988 |
|  | | (*in thousands*) | |
| Proceeds from Sales | $64,817 | $331,657 | $58,988 |
| Gross gains | $ 333 | $ 278 | $ 129 |
| Gross losses | $ 553 | $ 31,586 | $ 1,400 |

••••

DOWNEY SAVINGS AND LOAN ASSOCIATION, DECEMBER 31, 1990

*Notes to Consolidated Financial Statements*
*December 31, 1990, 1989, 1988*

Note 1—Summary of Significant Accounting Policies

••••

U.S. Government and Agency Obligations, Other Investment Securities and Mortgage-Backed Securities

The Association has established written guidelines and objectives for its investing activities. At the time of purchase of a U.S. Government and agency obligation, other investment security or a mortgage-backed security, management of the Association designates the security as either held for investment, sale or trading based on the Association's investment objectives, operational needs and intent. The Association then monitors its investment activities to assure that those activities are consistent with the established guidelines and objectives.

••••

Held for Investment

Securities held for investment are carried at cost, adjusted for amortization of premiums and accretion of discounts which are recognized in interest income using a method that approximates the level-yield method over the period to maturity. Mortgage-backed securities represent participating interests in pools of long-term first mortgage loans originated and serviced by the issuers of the securities. Mortgage-backed securities held for investment are carried at unpaid principal balances, adjusted for unamortized premiums and unearned discounts. Premiums and discounts on mortgage-backed securities are amortized using the level-yield method over the remaining period to contractual maturity, adjusted for anticipated prepayments. Management of the Association intends to hold such securities to maturity.

Held for Sale

Other investment securities and mortgage-backed securities held for sale are carried at the lower of cost or estimated market value in the aggregate. Net unrealized losses are recognized in a valuation allowance by charges to income.

Gains and losses on the sale of investment securities are determined using the specific identification method.

Note 2—U.S. Government and Agency Obligations and Other Investment Securities

The amortized cost and estimated market value of U.S. Government and agency obligations and other investment securities held for investment are summarized as follows:

| | Amortized Cost | Gross Unrealized Gains | Gross Unrealized Losses | Estimated Market Value |
|---|---|---|---|---|
| | | | (*in thousands*) | |
| **1990** | | | | |
| Held for investment: | | | | |
| U.S. Government and agency obligations | $334,858 | 836 | 22,487 | 313,207 |
| Investment grade corporate debt | 27,667 | — | 2,453 | 25,214 |
| Municipal bonds | 7,245 | — | 4 | 7,241 |
| Interest-only certificates | 20,633 | — | 1,967 | 18,666 |
| | $390,403 | 836 | 26,911 | 364,328 |
| **1989** | | | | |
| Held for investment: | | | | |
| U.S. Government and agency obligations | $355,290 | 178 | 16,079 | 339,389 |
| Investment grade corporate debt | 37,425 | — | 8,684 | 28,741 |
| Municipal bonds | 7,250 | — | 3 | 7,247 |
| Interest-only certificates | 23,792 | — | 2,793 | 20,999 |
| Other | 2,683 | — | 585 | 2,098 |
| | $426,440 | 178 | 28,144 | 398,474 |

The amortized cost and estimated market value of U.S. Government and agency obligations and other investment securities at December 31, 1990, by contractual maturity, are shown below. Expected maturities may differ from contractual maturities because certain borrowers may have the right to call or prepay obligations with or without call or prepayment penalties.

| | 1990 Amortized Cost | | | | |
|---|---|---|---|---|---|
| | Within 1 Year | After 1 Through 5 Years | After 5 Through 10 Years | Total After 10 Years | Amortized Cost |
| | | | (*in thousands*) | | |
| Held for investment: | | | | | |
| U.S. Government and agency obligations | $ 8,998 | 71,119 | 1,498 | 253,243 | 334,858 |
| Investment grade corporate debt | — | 100 | 2,859 | 24,708 | 27,667 |
| Municipal bonds | 7,000 | — | — | 245 | 7,245 |
| Interest-only certificates | — | — | 10,245 | 10,388 | 20,633 |
| | $15,998 | 71,219 | 14,602 | 288,584 | 290,403 |

48

|  | 1990 Estimated Market Value | | | | |
| --- | --- | --- | --- | --- | --- |
|  | Within 1 Year | After 1 Through 5 Years | After 5 Through 10 Years | After 10 Years | Total |
|  | | | *(in thousands)* | | |
| **Held for investment:** | | | | | |
| U. S. Government and agency obligations | $ 8,989 | 70,295 | 1,401 | 232,522 | 313,207 |
| Investment grade corporate debt | — | 96 | 2,579 | 22,539 | 25,214 |
| Municipal bonds | 7,000 | — | — | 241 | 7,241 |
| Interest-only certificates | — | — | 9,572 | 9,904 | 18,666 |
|  | $15,989 | 70,391 | 13,552 | 264,396 | 364,328 |

The other investment securities reflected separately on the December 31, 1990 consolidated balance sheet represent corporate debt held for sale that is due after ten years. Net unrealized losses on corporate debt held for sale recognized in a valuation allowance by charges to net gains (losses) on sales of investment securities for the year ended December 31, 1990 was $(3,589,000).

Proceeds, gross realized gains and gross realized losses from sales of U. S. Government and agency obligations and other investment securities were $47,736,000, $940,000 and $(1,271,000) for the year ended December 31, 1990, respectively.

Note 3—Mortgage-Backed Securities

The amortized cost and estimated market value of mortgage-backed securities held for investment or sale are summarized as follows:

|  | Amortized Cost | Gross Unrealized Gains | Gross Unrealized Losses | Estimated Market Value |
| --- | --- | --- | --- | --- |
|  | | *(in thousands)* | | |
| **1990** | | | | |
| **Held for investment:** | | | | |
| GNMA certificates | $ 32,747 | — | 1,772 | 30,975 |
| **Held for sale:** | | | | |
| GNMA certificates | $ 62,776 | 114 | 1,460 | 61,430 |
| FNMA certificates | 29,305 | 38 | 564 | 28,779 |
| FHLMC certificates | 22,622 | 63 | 604 | 22,081 |
| Collateralized mortgage obligations | 19,882 | — | 1,432 | 18,450 |
|  | $134,585 | 215 | 4,060 | 130,740 |
| **1989** | | | | |
| **Held for investments:** | | | | |
| GNMA certificates | $ 36,610 | — | 1,924 | 34,686 |
| FHLMC certificates | 4,796 | — | 47 | 4,749 |
|  | $ 41,406 | — | 1,971 | 39,435 |

*Mortgage-Backed Securities (continued)*

| | Amortized Cost | Gross Unrealized Gains | Gross Unrealized Losses | Estimated Market Value |
|---|---|---|---|---|
| | | *(in thousands)* | | |
| **Held for sale:** | | | | |
| GNMA certificates | $ 70,105 | 21 | 1,706 | 68,420 |
| FNMA certificates | 31,693 | — | 808 | 30,885 |
| FHLMC certificates | 20,391 | — | 700 | 19,691 |
| Collateralized mortgage obligations | 19,868 | — | 705 | 19,163 |
| | $142,057 | 21 | 3,919 | 138,159 |

Proceeds and gross realized gains from sales of mortgage-backed securities were $9,909,000 and $140,000 for the year ended December 31, 1990, respectively. Net unrealized gains (losses) on mortgage-backed securities held for sale recognized in a valuation allowance by charges to net gains (losses) on sales and loans and mortgage-backed securities for the years ended December 31, 1990 and 1989 were $53,000 and $(3,898,000), respectively.

GOLDOME, DECEMBER 31, 1990

*Goldome and Subsidiaries*
*Notes to Consolidated Financial Statements*
*December 31, 1990, 1989 and 1988*

1. Basis of Presentation and Summary of Significant Accounting Policies

• • • •

b. Investment Securities

Except as described below, investment securities are carried at cost, net of discounts and premiums, which are accreted or amortized to maturity using a method that approximates the interest method.... Gains and losses on sales of investments are determined using the specific identification method. No recognition has been given to the difference between the market and carrying values of investment securities carried at cost, as it is management's intention to hold such securities until maturity.

• • • •

c. Loans and Mortgage-Backed Securities

Loans and mortgage-backed securities are stated at principal balance, net of unearned discounts and premiums, which are accreted or amortized as interest income using a method that approximates the interest method over the estimated remaining lives of the loans and securities. No recognition has been given to the difference between the market values of mortgage-backed securities and their cost because Goldome has the ability to hold these securities until maturity and the intent to hold these securities for the forseeable future. However, through the action of Goldome's Asset/Liability Committee, mortgage-backed securities may be sold in order to manage interest-rate sensitivity.

• • • •

e. Mortgage Banking Activities

50

●●●●

Gains or losses on sales of mortgage loans and mortgage-backed securities are recognized at the time of settlement and are determined by the difference between net sales proceeds and the carrying value of the assets sold adjusted by the present value of the difference between estimated future net servicing revenues and normal servicing revenues (deferred excess service fees)....

4. Investment Securities

The carrying value of investment securities and their related estimated market value were:

| (in thousands) | December 31, 1990 | | December 31, 1989 | |
|---|---|---|---|---|
| | Carrying Value | Estimated Market Value | Carrying Value | Estimated Market Value |
| Bonds and Notes | | | | |
| U.S. Treasury securities | $ 27,525 | $ 27,563 | $ 47,432 | $ 46,840 |
| Other U.S. Government agencies and corporations | 5,788 | 5,786 | 5,775 | 5,712 |
| Other securities | 91,204 | 79,897 | 103,221 | 97,562 |
| Foreign securities | 2,750 | 2,750 | 2,250 | 2,250 |
| | 127,267 | 115,996 | 158,678 | 152,364 |
| | ●●●● | | | |
| | $153,289 | $142,018 | $199,718 | $187,459 |

●●●●

The following are summaries of unrealized and realized gains (losses) and sales proceeds on investment securities:

Unrealized gains (losses) were:

| (in thousands) | December 31 | |
|---|---|---|
| | 1990 | 1989 |
| Bonds and Notes: | | |
| Aggregate unrealized gains | $ 177 | $ 75 |
| Aggregate unrealized losses | (11,388) | (6,389) |
| | (11,271) | (6,314) |
| | ●●●● | |
| | $(20,039) | $(12,421) |

Realized gains (losses) were:

| (in thousands) | Years ended December 31 | | |
|---|---|---|---|
| | 1990 | 1989 | 1988 |
| Bonds and Notes: | | | |
| Aggregate realized gains | $ 730 | $ 7,110 | $ 18,246 |
| Aggregate realized losses | (319) | (54,104) | (16,749) |
| | 411 | (46,994) | 1,497 |

●●●●

*Investment Securities (continued)*

| (*in thousands*) | Years ended December 31 | | |
| --- | --- | --- | --- |
| | 1990 | 1989 | 1988 |
| | $(744) | $(57,290) | $ 1,314 |

Sale proceeds were:

| (*in thousands*) | Years ended December 31 | | |
| --- | --- | --- | --- |
| | 1990 | 1989 | 1988 |
| Bonds and notes | $ 9,615 | $1,355,652 | $1,201,037 |
| Equity securities | 5,872 | 62,964 | 113,486 |
| | $35,487 | $1,418,616 | $1,314,523 |

• • • •

The following summarizes the maturity distribution of investment securities at December 31, 1990:

| (*dollars in thousands*) | Due In One Year Or Less | | Due After One Through Five Years | |
| --- | --- | --- | --- | --- |
| | Amount | Yield | Amount | Yield |
| Carrying value and average yield: | | | | |
| U.S. Treasury securities | $22,509 | 7.54% | $ 5,016 | 7.22% |
| Other U.S. Government agencies and corporations | — | — | 4,400 | 6.97 |
| Other bonds and notes | 5,250 | 7.81 | 11,173 | 4.80 |
| Equity securities | — | — | — | — |
| | $27,759 | 7.59% | $20,589 | 5.85% |
| Estimated market value: | | | | |
| Bonds and notes | $27,799 | | $15,491 | |
| Equity securities | — | | — | |
| | $27,799 | | $15,491 | |

| (*dollars in thousands*) | Due After One Through Ten Years | | Due After Ten Years | |
| --- | --- | --- | --- | --- |
| | Amount | Yield | Amount | Yield |
| Carrying value and average yield: | | | | |
| U.S. Treasury securities | $ — | —% | $ — | —% |
| Other U.S. Government agencies and corporations | 1,388 | 9.05 | — | — |
| Other bonds and notes | 38,218 | 7.94 | 39,313 | 7.85 |
| Equity securities | — | — | 26,022 | 7.17 |
| | $39,606 | 7.98% | $65,335 | 7.58% |

| (dollars in thousands) | Due after one through ten years | | Due after ten years | |
|---|---|---|---|---|
| | Amount | Yield | Amount | Yield |
| **Estimated market value:** | | | | |
| Bonds and notes | $36,957 | | $35,749 | |
| Equity securities | — | | 26,022 | |
| | $36,957 | | $61,771 | |

| (dollars in thousands) | Total | |
|---|---|---|
| | Amount | Yield |
| **Carrying value and average yield:** | | |
| U.S. Treasury securities | $ 27,525 | 7.48% |
| Other U.S. Government agencies and corporations | 5,788 | 7.47 |
| Other bonds and notes | 93,954 | 7.52 |
| Equity securities | 26,022 | 7.17 |
| | $153,289 | 7.45% |
| **Estimated market value:** | | |
| Bonds and notes | $115,996 | |
| Equity securities | 26,022 | |
| | $142,018 | |

Stocks and other securities having no stated maturity are included in "Due After Ten Years".

5. Mortgage-Backed Securities

The mortgage-backed securities portfolio consisted of:

| (in thousands) | December 31 | |
|---|---|---|
| | 1990 | 1989 |
| GNMA | $ 218,828 | $ 461,639 |
| FHLMC | 545,279 | 652,685 |
| FNMA | 1,290,488 | 1,656,911 |
| Private issues | 1,178,784 | 1,205,643 |
| CMOs | 59,407 | 75,074 |
| | 3,292,786 | 4,051,952 |
| Less unearned discount | 21,816 | 41,805 |
| | $3,270,970 | $4,010,147 |

The carrying value of mortgage-backed securities consisted of $597,386,000 and $877,383,000 of fixed-rate and $2,695,400,000 and $3,174,569,000 of variable-rate securities at December 31, 1990 and 1989, respectively.

The following are summaries of unrealized and realized gains (losses) on mortgage-backed securities:

Unrealized gains (losses) were:

| (*in thousands*) | December 31 | |
|---|---|---|
| | 1990 | 1989 |
| Aggregate unrealized gains | $34,481 | $49,433 |
| Aggregate unrealized losses | (22,936) | (23,461) |
| | $11,545 | $25,972 |

Realized gains (losses) were:

| (*in thousands*) | Years ended December | | |
|---|---|---|---|
| | 1990 | 1989 | 1988 |
| Aggregate realized gains | $12,287 | $ 13,954 | $10,071 |
| Aggregate realized losses | (1,737) | (26,330) | (4,913) |
| | $10,550 | $(12,376) | $ 5,158 |

Sales proceeds of mortgage-backed securities were $707.2 million, $1.6 billion and $1.0 billion for the years ended December 31, 1990, 1989 and 1988, respectively.

HOWARD SAVINGS BANK, DECEMBER 31, 1990

*Notes to Consolidated Financial Statements*

1. Summary of Significant Accounting Policies

•  •  •  •

Investment and Mortgage-Backed Securities

Investment and mortgage-backed securities are carried at cost, adjusted for the amortization of premiums and accretion of discounts computed on a straight-line basis (which approximates the interest method) which are recognized as adjustments to interest income. These securities are recorded at amortized cost as it is the opinion of management that the Bank has the ability and intent to hold these securities to maturity. Gains and losses are recognized by the specific identification method when securities are sold.

Other Securities Held for Sale

Other securities held for sale are valued at the lower of cost or market on an aggregate portfolio basis. It is the intention of management to sell these securities in the near future. At December 31, 1990, other securities held for sale consisted entirely of mortgage-backed securities.

•  •  •  •

3. Investment Securities

The net book value of investment securities and the approximate market values were as follows:

| (*in thousands*) | December 31 | | | |
| --- | --- | --- | --- | --- |
| | 1990 | | 1989 | |
| | Net Book Value | Market Value | Net Book Value | Market Value |
| U.S. Treasury and other U.S. Government agencies: | | | | |
| Maturing within 1 year | $398,778 | $399,055 | $418,961 | $418,960 |
| Maturing between 1-5 years | 26,023 | 26,339 | 23,946 | 24,078 |
| Maturing between 5-10 years | 23,055 | 22,569 | 23,033 | 23,323 |
| | 447,856 | 447,963 | 465,940 | 465,361 |
| Obligations of states and political subdivisions: | | | | |
| Maturing within 1 year | 825 | 825 | 36,937 | 36,944 |
| Maturing between 1-5 years | 235 | 224 | 1,005 | 995 |
| Maturing between 5-10 years | 382 | 329 | 437 | 369 |
| Maturing after 10 years | 13,091 | 11,501 | 13,229 | 11,734 |
| | 14,533 | 12,879 | 51,608 | 50,042 |
| Other investment securities: | | | | |
| Maturing within 1 year | 48,842 | 48,969 | 50,470 | 50,572 |
| Maturing between 1-5 years | 193,075 | 192,676 | 75,690 | 74,844 |
| Maturing between 5-10 years | 47,180 | 42,287 | 56,923 | 51,288 |
| Maturing after 10 years | 39,379 | 34,370 | 46,515 | 41,339 |
| | 328,476 | 318,302 | 229,598 | 218,043 |
| | • • • • | | | |
| Total investment securities | $793,732 | $781,316 | $840,920 | $826,822 |

• • • •

The loss from security transactions and write-downs during 1990 was $2,139,000. Gross gains of $49,000 and gross losses of $2,188,000 were recognized on those transactions.

Gross unrealized gains and losses on investment securities are as follows at December 31, 1990:

| (*in thousands*) | Net Book Value | Gross Unrealized Gains | Gross Unrealized Losses | Estimated Market Value |
| --- | --- | --- | --- | --- |
| U.S. Treasury and other U.S. Government agencies | $447,856 | $ 578 | $ 471 | $447,963 |
| Obligations of states and other political subdivisions | 14,533 | — | 1,654 | 12,879 |
| Other investment securities | 328,476 | 987 | 11,161 | 318,302 |
| | • • • • | | | |
| Total investment securities | $793,732 | $1,565 | $13,981 | $781,316 |

There were no unrealized gains in the mortgage-backed securities portfolio at December 31, 1990.

•••

LANDMARK SAVINGS ASSOCIATION, DECEMBER 31, 1990

*Notes To Consolidated Financial Statements*

Note 1. Summary of Significant Accounting Policies

•••

Investment Securities

Securities are classified as either investment or trading securities when purchased using the specific identification method. The Company classifies securities as investment securities when it has the intent and ability to hold the securities to maturity. The Company classifies securities as trading securities when the intent is profit maximization through market appreciation and resale. No investment securities were held for trading purposes as of December 31, 1990 and 1989.

Investment securities are carried at cost and adjusted for amortization and accretion of premiums and discounts, net of an allowance for losses. Premiums and discount on investments are amortized and accreted to maturity using a method that approximates the interest method. The cost of investment securities sold is determined using the specific identification method.

Mortgage-Backed Securities and Loans Receivable

Mortgage-backed securities and loans receivable are stated at their unpaid balance including premiums and net of discounts and, in the case of loans receivable, net of allowances for credit losses. Interest on mortgage-backed securities and loans receivable is credited to income as earned and is accrued only if deemed collectible. Discounts and premiums on loans and mortgage-backed securities are accreted or amortized to income using the interest method over the estimated remaining terms of the loans adjusted for estimated prepayments. Loans and mortgage-backed securities are classified as held for investment based upon management's intent and ability to hold such assets until maturity. Loans and mortgage-backed securities identified for sale are valued at the lower of cost or market value on a net aggregate basis. The cost of loans and mortgage-backed securities sold is determined using the specific identification method.

Allowance for Estimated Losses

The allowance for loan and investment securities losses is available for future charge-offs. A general provision is made for losses on loans and investment securities based on management's review of prevailing economic conditions, delinquency trends, net loss experience, known and inherent risks in the portfolio, the estimated value of any underlying collateral and other factors. Landmark's loans and investment securities also are subject to regular review and examinations by an independent credit review group and by regulatory authorities. Additionally, allowances for losses on specific loans or investment securities are established when the carrying value exceeds estimated net realizable value. Management believes the allowances, when taken as a whole, are adequate to absorb reasonably foreseeable losses on loans and investment securities.

•••

Note 3. Investment Securities

A summary of investment securities at December 31 follows:

| (*dollars in thousands*) | Carrying Value | Gross Unrealized Gains | Gross Unrealized Losses | Market Value |
|---|---|---|---|---|
| **1990** | | | | |
| Corporate securities | $ 19,597 | $ 27 | $ (16) | $ 19,608 |
| Collateralized mortgage obligations (net of valuation allowance of $20) | 38,063 | 151 | (280) | 37,934 |
| U.S. Treasury securities | 1,996 | — | (5) | 1,991 |
| Federal agency securities | 4,100 | 8 | (1) | 4,107 |
| Interest-only securities (net of valuation allowance of $569) | 23,968 | 22 | (1,709) | 22,281 |
| REMIC residual securities (net of valuation allowance of $762) | 14,481 | 20 | (1,525) | 12,976 |
| Other securities | 2,371 | — | (122) | 2,249 |
| | $104,576 | $228 | $(3,658) | $101,146 |

| (*dollars in thousands*) | Carrying Value | Gross Unrealized Gains | Gross Unrealized Losses | Market Value |
|---|---|---|---|---|
| **1989** | | | | |
| Corporate securities | $ 9,375 | $12 | $ (61) | $ 9,326 |
| Collateralized mortgage obligations | 30,994 | 75 | (445) | 30,624 |
| U.S. Treasury securities | 1,990 | — | (39) | 1,951 |
| Federal agency securities | 4,104 | 9 | (39) | 4,074 |
| Interest-only securities | 28,669 | — | (4,079) | 24,590 |
| REMIC residual securities | 18,632 | — | (5,600) | 13,032 |
| Other securities | 2,651 | — | (197) | 2,454 |
| | $96,415 | $96 | $(10,460) | $86,051 |

The contractual maturities at December 31, 1990 are summarized in the following table. Based on actual and anticipated prepayments, the expected maturities are shorter than the contractual maturities.

| (*dollars in thousands*) | Carrying Value | Market Value |
|---|---|---|
| Due in one year or less | $ 7,391 | $ 7,388 |
| Due after one year through five years | 17,925 | 17,962 |
| Due after five years through ten years | 4,241 | 4,240 |
| Due after ten years | 75,019 | 71,556 |
| | $104,576 | $101,146 |

There were no trading securities held at December 31, 1990 or 1989.

Proceeds from sales of investments during 1990 were $7,314,000. Gross gains of $22,000 and gross losses of $11,000 were realized on these sales.

••••

Note 4. Mortgage-Backed Securities

A summary of mortgage-backed securities at December 31 follows:

| (*dollars in thousands*) | Carrying Value | Gross Unrealized Gains | Gross Unrealized Losses | Market Value |
|---|---|---|---|---|
| **1990** | | | | |
| Federal Home Loan Mortgage Corporation (FHLMC) | $126,927 | $ 499 | $(4,810) | $122,616 |
| Federal National Mortgage Association (FNMA) | 53,115 | 433 | (654) | 52,894 |
| Government National Mortgage Association (GNMA) | 16,119 | 284 | (349) | 16,054 |
| AA Rated Mortgage Certificates | 13,892 | 157 | (289) | 13,760 |
| Held for sale | 3,098 | 15 | — | 3,113 |
| | $213,151 | $1,388 | $(6,102) | $208,437 |

| (*dollars in thousands*) | Carrying Value | Gross Unrealized Gains | Gross Unrealized Losses | Market Value |
|---|---|---|---|---|
| **1989** | | | | |
| FHLMC | $170,308 | $ 717 | $(6,003) | $165,022 |
| FNMA | 59,614 | 251 | (1,034) | 58,831 |
| GNMA | 17,991 | 165 | (472) | 17,684 |
| AA Rated Mortgage Certificates | 12,805 | — | (308) | 12,497 |
| | $260,718 | $1,133 | $(7,817) | $254,034 |

Proceeds from sales of mortgage-backed securities during 1990 were $39,118,000. Gross gains of $805,000 and gross losses of $251,000 were realized on these sales.

Mortgage-backed securities included net unaccreted discount of $1,286,000 at December 31, 1990 and $680,000 at December 31, 1989. Accrued interest receivable on mortgage-backed securities was $2,519,000 and $3,441,000 at December 31, 1990 and 1989, respectively.

●●●●

# LIFE AND PROPERTY OR LIABILITY INSURANCE ENTERPRISES

In addition to banks, life and property or liability insurance enterprises also present information about debt securities in accordance with SOP 90-11. Examples of information disclosed in accordance with SOP 90-11 by seventeen enterprises that operate primarily in the field of life or property and liability insurance are presented below.

## LIFE INSURANCE ENTERPRISES

AETNA LIFE AND CASUALTY COMPANY, DECEMBER 31, 1990

*Notes to Financial Statements*

1.  Summary of Significant Accounting Policies

●●●●

Investments

Fixed maturity investments include bonds and redeemable preferred stocks and generally are carried at amortized cost, net of reserves. Fixed maturity investments which are traded with the objective of maximizing investment returns ("fixed maturity trading securities") are carried at market value and are included in fixed maturities. Bonds, redeemable preferred stocks and mortgage loans have maturities that generally match the insurance liabilities they support. The distribution of maturities in these fixed investments is monitored, and security purchases and sales are executed with the objective of having adequate funds available to satisfy the company's maturing insurance liabilities. Bonds and redeemable preferred stocks are recorded as purchases on the trade date. Mortgage loans are recorded as purchases on the closing date. Redeemable preferred stocks are expected to be retired as a result of regular sinking fund payments by the issuer.

••••

Realized capital gains or losses are the difference between cost and sales proceeds of specific investments sold. Realized capital gains or losses which are being credited (charged) to pension contractholders are not included in the Consolidated Statements of Income. Provision for impairments which are other than temporary are included in net realized capital gains or losses....

••••

4. Investments

Investments in fixed maturities were as follows:

| (*millions*) | Carrying Value | Gross Unrealized Gains | Gross Unrealized Losses | Market Value |
|---|---|---|---|---|
| 1990 | | | | |
| Fixed maturities: | | | | |
| Bonds: | | | | |
| U.S. Treasury securities and obligations of U.S. government agencies and corporations | $ 1,122.1 | $ 18.5 | $ 8.1 | $ 1,132.5 |
| Obligations of states and political subdivisions | 5,136.2 | 37.7 | 264.7 | 4,909.2 |
| Corporate securities | 14,195.0 | 558.1 | 165.6 | 14,587.5 |
| Mortgage pass-throughs | 9,701.2 | 396.3 | 57.9 | 10,039.6 |
| Other debt securities | 2,868.7 | 119.2 | 58.7 | 2,929.2 |
| | 33,023.2 | 1,129.8 | 555.0 | 33,598.0 |
| Fixed maturity trading securities | 998.4 | — | — | 998.4 |
| Total bonds | 34,021.6 | 1,129.8 | 555.0 | 34,596.4 |
| Redeemable preferred stock | 205.5 | 9.1 | 13.3 | 201.3 |
| Total fixed maturities | $34,227.1 | $1,138.9 | $568.3 | $34,797.7 |

The carrying value and market value of fixed maturities carried at amortized cost at December 31, 1990 are shown below by contractual maturity. Actual maturities will differ from contractual maturities because securities may be called or prepaid with or without call or prepayment penalties.

| (*millions*) | Carrying Value | Market Value |
|---|---|---|
| Due to mature: | | |
| One year or less | $1,827.4 | $ 1,827.4 |
| After one year through five years | 6,245.5 | 6,342.3 |
| After five years through ten years | 6,949.8 | 7,128.9 |
| After ten years | 8,504.8 | 8,461.1 |
| Mortgage pass-throughs | 9,701.2 | 10,039.6 |

Total fixed maturities carried

| (*millions*) | Carrying Value | Market Value |
|---|---|---|
| **1989** | | |
| Fixed maturities: | | |
| Bonds | $32,098.2 | $32,845.4 |
| Redeemable preferred stocks | 222.7 | 227.3 |
| | 32,320.9 | 33,072.7 |
| Fixed maturity trading securities: bonds | 930.6 | 930.6 |
| | $33,251.5 | $34,003.3 |

•  •  •  •

5.  Capital Gains and Losses on Investment Operations

Realized capital gains (losses) on investments were as follows:

| (*millions*) | 1990 | 1989 | 1988 |
|---|---|---|---|
| Fixed maturities: | | | |
| Bonds | $ (35.1) | $  1.1 | $17.6 |
| Redeemable preferred stocks | .9 | (.6) | 14.2 |

•  •  •  •

| | 1990 | 1989 | 1988 |
|---|---|---|---|
| | $(126.2) | $246.0 | $43.5 |
| Realized capital gains (losses), net of tax | $ (81.7) | $109.0 | $31.2 |

Proceeds from sales of investments in fixed maturities carried at amortized cost during 1990 were $3,680.9 million. Gross gains of $43.3 million and gross losses of $66.1 million were realized on those sales.

•  •  •  •

Changes in unrealized capital gains (losses) for the periods exclude pretax changes in fixed maturities carried at amortized cost. Such unrecorded appreciation (depreciation) is the difference between estimated market and carrying values, and amounted to approximately $(.2) billion, $1.6 billion and $(.6) billion in 1990, 1989 and 1988, respectively.

AMERICAN FAMILY CORPORATION, DECEMBER 31, 1990

*Notes to Consolidated Financial Statements*

(1)  Summary of Significant Accounting Policies

•  •  •  •

Investments: Fixed-maturity investments (principally bonds) are securities which mature at a specified future date more than one year after they were issued and are generally presented at amortized cost. Amortized cost is based on the purchase price, adjusted periodically, in order that the carrying value will equal the face or par value at maturity....

• • • •

Realized Investment Gains or Losses: Gains and losses on the sale or maturity of investments, together with provisions for possible losses on investments with permanent declines in value or investments for which disposition decisions have been made, are included in realized investment gains (losses) in the consolidated statements of earnings. Costs of securities sold are determined on the first-in, first-out method.

• • • •

(3) Investments

The amortized cost and estimated market values of investments in fixed-maturity securities at December 31, 1990, were as follows:

| (in thousands) | Amortized Cost | Gross Unrealized Gains | Gross Unrealized Losses | Estimated Market Value |
|---|---|---|---|---|
| Yen-denominated bonds: | | | | |
| Japan National Government direct obligations | $1,248,951 | $ 5,033 | $ 77,070 | $1,176,914 |
| Japan Government guaranteed | 501,939 | 3,110 | 11,642 | 493,407 |
| Japan municipalities | 496,634 | 4,337 | 13,126 | 487,885 |
| Japan public utilities | 1,204,567 | 5,698 | 58,866 | 1,151,399 |
| Corporate obligations: | | | | |
| Banks and other financial institutions | 205,510 | 412 | 5,398 | 200,524 |
| Foreign issuers (Euroyen and Samurai) | 1,182,279 | 2,281 | 90,753 | 1,093,807 |
| Other | 157,830 | — | 1,814 | 156,016 |
| | 4,997,710 | 20,911 | 258,669 | 4,759,952 |
| U.S. dollar securities: | | | | |
| U.S. Government direct obligations | 235,139 | 6,286 | 268 | 241,157 |
| U.S. agencies (FNMA, etc.) | 73,489 | 1,879 | 360 | 75,008 |
| U.S. mortgage-backed securities (GNMA) | 10,541 | 13 | 485 | 10,069 |
| Corporate obligations | 589,434 | 7,554 | 7,219 | 589,769 |
| | 908,603 | 15,732 | 8,332 | 916,003 |
| Other foreign securities | 16,089 | — | 119 | 15,970 |
| Total fixed-maturity securities | $5,922,402 | $36,643 | $267,120 | $5,691,925 |

The amortized cost and estimated market value of fixed-maturity securities at December 31, 1990, by contractual maturity are shown below:

62

| (*in thousands*) | Amortized Cost | Estimated Market Value |
|---|---|---|
| Due in one year or less | $ 145,759 | $ 145,627 |
| Due after one year through five years | 1,345,182 | 1,336,799 |
| Due after five years through 10 years | 3,386,205 | 3,202,849 |
| Due after 10 years | 1,034,715 | 996,581 |
| | 5,911,861 | 5,681,856 |
| U.S. mortgage-backed securities (GNMA) | 10,541 | 10,069 |
| | $5,922,402 | $5,691,925 |

Expected maturities will differ from contractual maturities because issuers may have the right to call or prepay obligations with or without call or prepayment penalties.

Proceeds from sales of investments in fixed-maturity securities prior to their scheduled maturity dates were $320.1 million in 1990, $640.0 million in 1989 and $712.1 million in 1988.

Realized and unrealized gains and losses from investments for the years ended December 31 were as follows:

| (*in thousands*) | 1990 | 1989 | 1988 |
|---|---|---|---|
| Realized gains (losses) on sale or maturity of investments: | | | |
| Fixed-maturity securities: | | | |
| Gross gains from sales | $ 3,157 | $ 10,265 | $13,931 |
| Gross losses from sales | (5,096) | (3,945) | (8,686) |
| Net gains from redemptions | 306 | 282 | 284 |
| Net gains (losses) | (1,633) | 6,602 | 5,529 |

• • • •

| | 1990 | 1989 | 1988 |
|---|---|---|---|
| Net realized gains | 407 | 5,834 | 3,237 |
| Changes in unrealized gains (losses): | | | |
| Fixed-maturity securities | (208,181) | (185,980) | 43,636 |

• • • •

| | 1990 | 1989 | 1988 |
|---|---|---|---|
| Net unrealized gains (losses) | (217,853) | (178,202) | 57,543 |
| Combined realized and unrealized gains (losses) | $(217,446) | $(172,368) | $60,780 |

• • • •

.... Investments in fixed-maturity securities are carried at amortized cost in the financial statements. Therefore, the above unrealized gains and losses for fixed-maturity securities are not reflected in the financial statements but are presented above for information purposes.

• • • •

63

AMERICAN GENERAL CORPORATION, DECEMBER 31, 1990

*Notes to Financial Statements*

1. Accounting Policies

• • • •

1.2 Investments

Fixed Maturities.

Fixed maturity investments are securities that mature more than one year after they were issued. This balance sheet classification includes bonds, notes receivable, and preferred stocks with mandatory redemption features. All fixed maturities are considered held for investment purposes and, therefore, are carried at amortized cost, adjusted for declines considered other than temporary and for possible uncollectible amounts. The difference between amortized cost and the estimated market value of these investments is not reflected in the financial statements (see Note 2.3).

• • • •

Realized Gains or Losses.

When an investment is sold, its selling price may be higher or lower than its cost. The difference between the selling price and cost is recorded as a gain or loss (using the specific identification method) in the realized investment gains account on the Consolidated Statement of Income. If the value of an investment declines below its cost or amortized cost and this decline is considered to be other than temporary, the investment is reduced to its net realizable value, and the reduction is recorded as a realized loss.

• • • •

2. Investments

• • • •

2.2 Realized Investment Gains

Realized gains by type of investment were as follows:

| (*in millions*) | 1990 | 1989 | 1988 |
|---|---|---|---|
| Fixed maturities | | | |
| Gross gain | $ 35 | $ 21 | $ 65 |
| Gross losses | (140) | (24) | (90) |
| Total fixed maturities | (105) | (3) | (25) |

• • • •

| | | | |
|---|---|---|---|
| Net realized gains before taxes | 185 | 54 | 38 |
| Income tax expense | 69 | 24 | 15 |
| Net realized gains | $ 116 | $ 30 | $ 23 |

## 2.3 Fixed Maturities

Amortized cost and related estimated market value information were as follows:

(*in millions*)

| | Amortized Cost | | |
|---|---|---|---|
| | 1990 | 1989 | 1988 |
| **Bonds and notes** | | | |
| **Corporate securities:** | | | |
| Investment grade | $ 8,495 | $ 8,165 | $ 7,576 |
| Below investment grade (*) | 811 | 1,045 | 947 |
| Mortgage-backed securities (**) | 5,306 | 3,743 | 3,091 |
| U.S. Government obligations | 383 | 394 | 410 |
| Foreign governments | 366 | 255 | 246 |
| States and political subdivisions | 141 | 149 | 154 |
| Redeemable preferred stocks | 82 | 59 | 50 |
| Total | $15,584 | $13,810 | $12,474 |

| | Gross Unrealized Gain | | |
|---|---|---|---|
| | 1990 | 1989 | 1988 |
| **Bonds and notes** | | | |
| **Corporate securities:** | | | |
| Investment grade | $226 | $254 | $132 |
| Below investment grade (*) | 16 | 16 | 49 |
| Mortgage-backed securities (**) | 193 | 165 | 70 |
| U.S. Government obligations | 17 | 20 | 10 |
| Foreign governments | 17 | 18 | 12 |
| States and political subdivisions | 18 | 18 | 14 |
| Redeemable preferred stocks | 3 | 8 | 9 |
| Total | $490 | $499 | $296 |

| | Gross Unrealized Loss | | |
|---|---|---|---|
| | 1990 | 1989 | 1988 |
| **Bonds and notes** | | | |
| **Corporate securities:** | | | |
| Investment grade | $(140) | $(108) | $(280) |
| Below investment grade (*) | (78) | (80) | (31) |
| Mortgage-backed securities (**) | (33) | (23) | (100) |
| U.S. Government obligations | (9) | (4) | (23) |
| Foreign governments | (2) | (1) | (4) |
| States and political subdivisions | — | — | (1) |
| Redeemable preferred stocks | (2) | (4) | (3) |
| Total | $(264) | $(220) | $(442) |

*Fixed Maturities (continued)*

|  | Market Value | | |
|---|---|---|---|
|  | 1990 | 1989 | 1988 |
| Bonds and notes | | | |
| Corporate securities: | | | |
| Investment grade | $ 8,581 | $ 8,311 | $ 7,428 |
| Below investment grade (*) | 749 | 981 | 965 |
| Mortgage-backed securities (**) | 5,466 | 3,885 | 3,061 |
| U.S. Government obligations | 391 | 410 | 397 |
| Foreign governments | 381 | 272 | 254 |
| States and political subdivisions | 159 | 167 | 167 |
| Redeemable preferred stocks | 83 | 63 | 56 |
| Total | $15,810 | $14,089 | $12,328 |

(*) The 1990 amounts are net of a $43 million allowance for losses.

(**) Primarily included pass-through securities guaranteed by and mortgage obligations (CMOs) collateralized by the U.S. Government and government agencies.

Fixed maturity investments are not intended to be sold in the normal course of business and are usually held until maturity. Therefore, the presentation without a corresponding revaluation of related policyholder liabilities can be misinterpreted, and care should be exercised in drawing conclusions from such data.

The contractual maturities of fixed maturity investments at December 31, 1990, were as follows:

(*in millions*)

|  | Amortized Cost | Market Value |
|---|---|---|
| Fixed maturities, excluding mortgage-backed securities | | |
| Due in one year or less | $ 121 | $ 123 |
| Due after one through five years | 1,595 | 1,615 |
| Due after five years through ten years | 4,773 | 4,776 |
| Due after ten years | 3,789 | 3,830 |
| Mortgage-backed securities | 5,306 | 5,466 |
| Total | $15,584 | $15,810 |

Expected maturities will differ from contractual maturities as borrowers may have the right to call or prepay obligations with or without call or prepayment penalties. Proceeds from sales of fixed maturities were $1.6 billion, $631 million, and $987 million during 1990, 1989 and 1988, respectively.

●●●●

66

AMERICAN HERITAGE LIFE INVESTMENT CORPORATION, DECEMBER 31, 1990

*Notes to Consolidated Financial Statements*

(1) Summary of Significant Accounting Policies

•••••

(c) Valuation of Certain Investments

Fixed maturity investments are securities which mature at a specified future date more than one year after they were issued and are generally stated at amortized cost.... Realized investment gains or losses are calculated on the basis of specific identification. No provision has been made for the excess of cost over market value on investments in fixed maturities since the Company generally intends to hold such investments to maturity and does not expect to realize any significant losses....

•••••

(3) Investments

•••••

Realized gains (losses) on investments during the three years ended December 31, 1990 are summarized as follows:

|  | 1990 | 1989 | 1988 |
|---|---|---|---|
| Fixed maturities | $(388,075) | 142,752 | (77,823) |

•••••

| Realized gains (losses) | $(535,196) | (473,325) | (920,218) |

For the year ended December 31, 1990, gross gains of $3,434,204 and gross losses of $3,331,039 were realized on sales of fixed maturities.

Unrealized appreciation (depreciation) in investments for each of the years in the three year period ended December 31, 1990 are detailed below:

|  | 1990 | 1989 | 1988 |
|---|---|---|---|

•••••

| Fixed maturities | (4,992,338) | 10,235,956 | (649,110) |
| Net unrealized gain (loss) | $(5,699,219) | 14,573,841 | 661,096 |

The amortized cost and estimated market values of investments in fixed maturities by categories of securities are as follows:

|  | Amortized Cost | Gross Unrealized Gains | Gross Unrealized Losses | Estimated Market Value |
|---|---|---|---|---|
| December 31, 1990: | | | | |
| Obligations of U.S. government corporations and agencies | $ 7,533,489 | 899,846 | — | 8,433,335 |
| Obligations of state and local governments | 5,414,998 | 336,065 | — | 5,751,063 |
| Corporate securities | 72,898,985 | 912,069 | 6,067,798 | 67,743,256 |
| GNMA's | 211,920,409 | 6,653,897 | 665,268 | 217,909,038 |
| Total | $297,767,881 | 8,801,877 | 6,733,066 | 299,836,692 |
| December 31, 1989: | | | | |
| Obligations of U.S. government corporations and agencies | $ 7,578,559 | 1,033,263 | — | 8,611,822 |
| Obligations of state and local governments | 5,564,934 | 500,141 | — | 6,065,075 |
| Corporate securities | 96,133,428 | 4,150,344 | 1,870,904 | 98,412,868 |
| GNMA's | 157,274,971 | 3,503,971 | 255,666 | 160,523,276 |
| Total | $266,551,892 | 9,187,719 | 2,126,570 | 273,613,041 |

The amortized cost and estimated market value of fixed maturities at December 31, 1990, by contractual maturity, are as follows. Expected maturities will differ from contractual maturities because borrowers may have the right to call or repay obligations with or without penalties.

|  | December 31, 1990 | |
|---|---|---|
|  | Amortized Cost | Estimated Market Value |
| Due in one year or less | $ 2,147,989 | 2,213,125 |
| Due after one year through five years | 13,919,891 | 14,552,262 |
| Due after five years through ten years | 20,293,006 | 18,428,885 |
| Due after ten years | 42,341,708 | 40,420,521 |
| GNMA's | 211,920,409 | 217,909,038 |
| Redeemable preferred stock | 7,144,878 | 6,312,861 |
| Total | $297,767,881 | 299,836,692 |

AMERICAN NATIONAL INSURANCE COMPANY, DECEMBER 31, 1990

*Notes to Consolidated Financial Statements*

(1) Summary of significant accounting policies

•••

Valuation of Investments—Investments are reported on the following bases:

Bonds and redeemable preferred stocks are carried at amortized cost, less allowance for possible losses.

•••

When the value of an investment is considered to be permanently impaired, the decrease in value is recognized currently as a realized investment loss.

The market values of bonds and stocks represent quoted market values from published sources or calculated market values using the "yield method" if no quoted market values are obtainable.

Income from Investments—

The cost of investments sold is determined on the specific identification method.

•••

(2) Investment operations

The carrying value of bonds and redeemable preferred stocks (which have the characteristics of debt securities) is expected to be realized because management intends to hold these securities until maturity. Common stocks and non-redeemable preferred stocks are carried at market. The gross unrealized gains and gross unrealized losses at December 31, were as follows (*in thousands*):

|  | 1990 | 1989 |
|---|---|---|
| Unrealized gains | $144,659 | $154,241 |
| Unrealized losses | (39,851) | (23,154) |
|  | $104,808 | $131,087 |
| Provision for federal income taxes | (34,594) | (42,611) |
|  | $ 70,213 | $ 88,476 |

•••

The realized gains (losses) on investments before federal income taxes for the years ended December 31, are summarized as follows (*in thousands*):

|  | 1990 | 1989 |
|---|---|---|
| Bonds | $(18,877) | $ (676) |
| Preferred stocks | (49) | (144) |

•••

|  | 1990 | 1989 |
|---|---|---|
|  | $ 30,226 | $100,243 |
| Increase in allowances for losses | (10,025) | (19,902) |
|  | $ 20,201 | $ 80,341 |

•••

(4) Investment in debt securities

The amortized cost and estimated market values of investments in debt securities at December 31, 1990 are as follows (*in thousands*):

69

|  | Amortized Cost | Gross Unrealized Gains | Gross Unrealized Losses | Estimated Market Value |
|---|---|---|---|---|
| **Bonds:** | | | | |
| US Treasury securities and obligations of US government corporations and agencies | $ 18,592 | $ 509 | $ (147) | $ 18,954 |
| Obligations of states and political subdivisions | 23,398 | 341 | (719) | 23,020 |
| Debt securities issued by foreign governments | 59,555 | 241 | (1,575) | 58,221 |
| Corporate securities | 1,197,211 | 18,048 | (35,479) | 1,179,780 |
| Mortgage-backed securities | 517,466 | 14,466 | (731) | 531,201 |
| Other debt securities | 26,448 | 267 | (1,531) | 25,184 |
| | $1,842,670 | $33,872 | $(40,182) | $1,836,360 |
| **Redeemable Preferred Stock:** | | | | |
| Corporate Securities | $ 6,722 | $ 1 | $ (1,714) | $ 5,009 |

The amortized cost and estimated market value of debt securities at December 31, 1990 by contractual maturity, are shown below. Expected maturities will differ from contractual maturities because borrowers may have the right to call or prepay obligations with or without call or prepayment penalties.

|  | Amortized Cost | Estimated Market Value |
|---|---|---|
| **Bonds:** | | |
| Due in one year or less | $ 18,388 | $ 17,436 |
| Due after one year through five years | 556,300 | 558,973 |
| Due after five years through ten years | 558,214 | 549,951 |
| Due after 10 years | 672,692 | 672,475 |
| | $1,805,594 | $1,798,835 |
| Without single maturity date | 37,076 | 37,525 |
| | $1,842,670 | $1,836,360 |
| **Redeemable Preferred Stocks:** | | |
| Due after five years through ten years | $ 1,976 | $ 1,294 |
| Due after 10 years | 349 | 266 |
| | $ 2,325 | $ 1,560 |
| Without single maturity date | 4,397 | 3,449 |
| | $ 6,722 | $ 5,009 |

Proceeds from sales of investment in bonds during 1990 were $141,002,000. Gross gains of $4,127,000 and gross losses of $23,004,000 were realized on those sales.

Proceeds from sales of investment in redeemable preferred stocks during 1990 were $465,000. Gross gains of $2,000 were realized on those sales.

AON CORPORATION, DECEMBER 31, 1990

*Notes to Consolidated Financial Statements*

1. Summary of Significant Accounting Principles and Practices

•• ••

Investments

In the consolidated statements of financial position, fixed income securities and mortgages are carried generally at amortized cost, reflecting Aon's policy of holding such instruments to maturity. However, in cases where there are changes in the business or financial fundamentals, individual securities may be liquidated prior to maturity.... Realized investment gains or losses are computed using specific costs of securities sold.

Investments that have declines in market value below cost, and the decline is judged to be other than temporary, are written down to estimated fair values.... Writedowns....are included in realized investment gains and losses in the statements of income.

•• ••

3. Investments

•• ••

Realized gains (losses) on investments are as follows:

| (*millions*) | Years ended December 31 | | |
| --- | --- | --- | --- |
| | 1990 | 1989 | 1988 |
| Fixed maturities | $(6.4) | $(8.9) | $ 6.7 |

•• ••

| | | | |
| --- | --- | --- | --- |
| Total before tax | 4.9 | 4.2 | (41.2) |
| Less applicable tax | 1.3 | 1.1 | 16.4 |
| Total | $ 3.6 | $ 3.1 | $(24.8) |

Market fluctuations on fixed maturity investments are not reflected in the consolidated financial statements. The amortized cost and market values of investments in fixed maturities as of December 31, 1990 are as follows:

| (*millions*) | Amortized Cost | Gross Unrealized Gains | Gross Unrealized Losses | Market Value |
| --- | --- | --- | --- | --- |
| US Treasury securities and obligations of other US government agencies and corporations | $ 449.9 | $ 7.4 | $ (2.5) | $ 454.8 |
| Obligations of U.S. states and political subdivisions | 744.2 | 31.1 | ( .9) | 774.4 |

*Investments (continued)*

| (*millions*) | Amortized Cost | Gross Unrealized Gains | Gross Unrealized Losses | Market Value |
|---|---|---|---|---|
| Debt securities of foreign governments not classified as loans | 437.6 | 8.0 | (8.8) | 436.8 |
| Corporate securities | 2,671.5 | 37.9 | (77.8) | 2,631.6 |
| Mortgage-backed securities | 1,013.0 | 22.5 | ( .7) | 1,034.8 |
| Other fixed maturities | 51.5 | .4 | (2.9) | 49.0 |
| Total | $5,367.7 | $107.3 | $(93.6) | $5,381.4 |

The change in net unrealized gains (losses) on fixed maturities in 1990, 1989 and 1988 was ($27.5) million, $107.3 million and ($17.1) million, respectively. The amortized cost and market value of fixed maturities at December 31, 1990, by contractual maturity, are shown below. Expected maturities will differ from contractual maturities because borrowers may have the right to call or prepay obligations with or without call or prepayment penalties.

| (*millions*) | Amortized Cost | Market Value |
|---|---|---|
| Due in one year or less | $  108.9 | $  108.5 |
| Due after one year through five years | 1,182.4 | 1,187.1 |
| Due after five years through ten years | 1,862.2 | 1,872.0 |
| Due after ten years | 2,214.2 | 2,213.8 |
| Total | $5,367.7 | $5,381.4 |

Proceeds from sales of investments in fixed maturities during 1990 were $979.2 million. Gross gains of $15.9 million and gross losses of $22.3 million were realized on those sales.

•  •  •  •

CAPITAL HOLDING CORPORATION, DECEMBER 31, 1990

*Notes to Consolidated Financial Statements*

Note A—Significant Accounting Policies

•  •  •  •

Investments

Bonds and redeemable preferred stocks are purchased and held as long as their relative value is consistent with the underlying asset/liability strategy under which the purchase was made. They are carried at cost adjusted for amortization of premium and accretion of discount....

•  •  •  •

Net income includes realized gains and losses on investments sold and provisions for impairment in value of investments retained. The cost of investments sold is determined on a first-in, first-out basis....

72

•••• 

Note C—Investments

See the table on page 28 for the cost, market and carrying values for bonds and redeemable preferred stocks and common and nonredeemable preferred stocks at December 31, 1990, 1989 and 1988, the annual change in net unrealized investment gain or loss and the amount of realized investment gain or loss included in net income, for the respective years then ended. [*Ed. Note: Table 28 is omitted from this survey.*] Additionally, the tables below contain amortized cost and market value information on debt securities by various categories at December 31, 1990:

| (dollars in thousands) | Amortized Cost | Gross Unrealized Gains | Gross Unrealized Losses | Market Value |
|---|---|---|---|---|
| US Government obligations | $ 612,746 | $ 3,494 | $ 12,231 | $ 604,009 |
| States and political subdivisions | 354,645 | 8,089 | 2,008 | 360,726 |
| Corporate | 4,359,523 | 105,060 | 106,563 | 4,358,920 |
| Mortgage-backed | 1,798,045 | 45,965 | 46,629 | 1,794,381 |
| Other | 235,260 | 11,368 | 5,733 | 240,895 |
| Total | $7,360,219 | $174,876 | $176,164 | $7,358,931 |

The amortized cost and market value of debt securities at December 31, 1990, by contractual maturity, are shown below. Expected maturities will differ from contractual maturities because borrowers may have the right to call or prepay obligations, sometimes without call or prepayment penalties.

| (dollars in thousands) | Amortized Cost | Market Value |
|---|---|---|
| Due in one year or less | $ 116,780 | $ 117,090 |
| Due after one year through five years | 802,406 | 803,618 |
| Due after five years through ten years | 1,171,597 | 1,161,422 |
| Due after ten years | 3,471,391 | 3,482,420 |
| Subtotal | 5,562,174 | 5,564,550 |
| Mortgage-backed securities | 1,798,045 | 1,794,381 |
| Total | $7,360,219 | $7,358,931 |

Proceeds during 1990 from sales of investments in debt securities were $11,342,794,000. Gross gains of $118,273,000 and gross losses of $174,779,000 were realized on those sales.

•••• 

FIRST CAPITAL HOLDINGS CORP., DECEMBER 31, 1990

*Notes to Consolidated Financial Statements*

December 31, 1990, 1989 and 1988

2.  Summary of Significant Accounting Policies

••••

Investments:

Fixed maturities (bonds, notes and redeemable preferred stocks) are recorded at cost, adjusted for amortization of premium or discount as the Company has the intent and ability to hold them to maturity....

Realized investment gains and losses, determined on the basis of specific identification, are included in net income....

The Company recognizes losses on its high-yield and non-investment grade bonds when it is probable that the cost of an asset has been impaired and the decline in value is other than temporary. The amortized cost of the asset is then reduced to its estimated net realizable value, which is based upon an estimate of the recovery of the amortized cost of the investment. The Company does not discount expected future cash flows in the computation of net realizable values. While the Company uses many sources of available information to estimate the net realizable value, further reductions of the Company's estimates may be necessary based on future events such as changes in economic conditions. Once the amortized cost of a publicly traded fixed maturity is reduced for a decline in net realizable value, the security is assigned a new cost basis. Any subsequent recoveries in net realizable value are not recognized until realized.

•••• 

3. Investments

On February 12, 1991, the Company released to the public its earnings for the fourth quarter and the year. Events related to high-yield bonds owned by the Company, subsequent to the earnings release date and prior to the issuance of the financial statements, resulted in a reduction in the estimated net realizable value of certain of the Company's investments by $ 33.0 million net of applicable income taxes. Additionally, in accordance with the Company's policy, $ 1.8 million of accrued interest related to these securities was written off. The subsequent event has been reflected as a reduction to net income from that originally reported in the Company's earnings release of February 12, 1991.

•••• 

The amortized cost and estimated market value of investments in debt securities are as follows:

| (in thousands) | Amortized Cost | Gross Unrealized Gains | Gross Unrealized Losses | Estimated Market Value |
|---|---|---|---|---|
| US Treasury securities and obligations of US government corporations and agencies | $1,234,806 | $11,734 | $ 5,400 | $1,241,140 |
| Obligations of states and political subdivisions | 8,842 | 15 | 366 | 8,491 |
| Debt securities issued by foreign governments | 1,075 | 62 | 7 | 1,130 |
| Corporate securities | 4,168,018 | 17,942 | 847,441 | 3,338,519 |
| Mortgage-backed securities | 433,621 | 6,418 | 3,933 | 436,106 |
| Other debt securities | 18,472 | | 10,113 | 8,359 |
| Reduction to net realizable value | (138,500) | | | |
| Total | $5,726,334 | $36,171 | $867,260 | $5,033,745 |

Included above are investments with an amortized cost of $1,122,717,000 which are not publicly traded.

••••

The amortized cost and estimated market value of debt securities at December 31, 1990, by contractual maturity, are shown below. Expected maturities will differ from contractual maturities because borrowers may have the right to call or prepay obligations with or without call or prepayment penalties.

| (in thousands) | Amortized Cost | Market Value |
|---|---|---|
| Due in one year or less | $ 131,878 | $ 112,609 |
| Due after 1 through 5 years | 931,757 | 789,615 |
| Due after 5 through 10 years | 2,507,611 | 1,946,894 |
| Due after 10 years | 643,997 | 524,863 |
| Mortgage-backed securities | 1,649,591 | 1,659,764 |
| Reduction to net realizable value | (138,500) | |
| | $5,726,334 | $5,033,745 |

Proceeds from sales of investments in debt securities during 1990 were $3,748,022,000. Gross gains of $51,660,000 and gross losses of $116,575,000, including a $112,000,000 reduction to the net realizable value of investments, were reflected in net gains (losses) from investments included in the Consolidated Statement of Income.

••••

Realized gains and losses, and the change in unrealized gains and losses on fixed maturity and equity securities, are summarized below:

| (in thousands) | Fixed Maturities | Equity Securities | Mortgage Loans and Other | Net Gain (Loss) |
|---|---|---|---|---|
| **1990** | | | | |
| Realized | $ (64,915) | $ 1,619 | $ (4,585) | $ (67,881) |
| Unrealized | (500,700) | (7,035) | | (507,735) |
| **1989** | | | | |
| Realized | 5,332 | (135) | (1,841) | 3,356 |
| Unrealized | (85,126) | (3,605) | | (88,731) |
| **1988** | | | | |
| Realized | 8,494 | 844 | 244 | 9,582 |
| Unrealized | (57,285) | 2,063 | | (55,222) |

••••

# PROPERTY AND LIABILITY INSURANCE ENTERPRISES

AMERICAN INTERNATIONAL GROUP INC., DECEMBER 31, 1990

*American International Group, Inc. and subsidiaries*
*Notes to Financial Statements*

1.  Summary of Significant Accounting Policies

• • • •

(c) Investments in Fixed Maturities and Equity Securities:

Bonds and redeemable preferred stocks are carried at amortized cost when it is the intent to hold the securities for the foreseeable future. Where fixed maturity investments are held for trading purposes, they are carried at market values; common and other preferred stocks are carried at market values.... Realized capital gains and losses are determined by specific identification.

8.  Investment Information

• • • •

(c) Investment Gains and Losses:

The realized capital gains and change in unrealized appreciation of investments for 1990, 1989 and 1988 are summarized below:

(*in thousands*)
Years Ended December 31,

|                                                   | 1990     | 1989      | 1988     |
| ------------------------------------------------- | -------- | --------- | -------- |
| Realized capital gains (losses) on investments:   |          |           |          |
| Fixed maturities (a)                              | $ 3,856  | $ 34,341  | $20,724  |
| • • • •                                           |          |           |          |
| Realized capital gains                            | $99,395  | $123,693  | $61,078  |

• • • •

(a) Including trading portfolios.

Proceeds from sales of investments in fixed maturities carried at amortized cost during 1990 were $3,209,586,000. Gross gains of $45,855,000 and gross losses of $29,044,000 were realized on those sales.

(d)  Market Value of Fixed Maturities and Unrealized Appreciation of Investments:

Bonds with an amortized cost of $18,446,538,000 had a quoted market value of $18,524,417,000 at December 31, 1990. Market valuations were not readily available for foreign bonds with an amortized cost of $370,764,000....

• • • •

The amortized cost and estimated market values of investments in fixed maturities carried at amortized cost at December 31, 1990 are as follows:

| (in thousands) | Amortized Cost | Gross Unrealized Gains | Gross Unrealized Losses | Market Value |
|---|---|---|---|---|
| Fixed maturities: | | | | |
| Bonds: | | | | |
| United States Government and government agencies and authorities | $    142,948 | $ 25,854 | $   3,631 | $    165,171 |
| States, municipalities and political subdivisions | 9,389,600 | 262,688 | 33,225 | 9,619,063 |
| Foreign governments | 1,849,537 | 11,473 | 18,764 | 1,842,246 |
| All other corporate | 7,435,217 | 56,048 | 222,564 | 7,268,701 |
| Total bonds | 18,817,302 | 356,063 | 278,184 | 18,895,181 |
| Redeemable preferred stocks | 203,655 | 703 | 4,494 | 199,864 |
| Total fixed maturities | $19,020,957 | $356,766 | $282,678 | $19,095,045 |

The amortized cost and estimated market value of fixed maturities at December 31, 1990, by contractual maturity, are shown below. Actual maturities could differ from contractual maturities because borrowers may have the right to call or prepay obligations with or without call or prepayment penalties.

| (in thousands) | Amortized Cost | Estimated Market Value |
|---|---|---|
| Due in one year or less | $    828,152 | $    815,424 |
| Due after one year through five years | 4,042,228 | 4,057,470 |
| Due after five years through ten years | 5,623,759 | 5,678,643 |
| Due after ten years | 8,526,818 | 8,543,508 |
| Total | $19,020,957 | $19,095,045 |

●●●●

AMERICAN RELIANCE GROUP INC., DECEMBER 31, 1990

*Notes to Consolidated Financial Statements*

1. Summary of Significant Accounting Policies

●●●●

Fixed maturities are carried at amortized cost.... Realized investment gains and losses, computed using the specific cost method, are included in the determination of income....

2. Investments

Invested assets at December 31 were as follows:

| (in thousands) | Cost | Gross Unrealized Gains | Gross Unrealized Losses | Market Value |
|---|---|---|---|---|
| **1990** | | | | |
| Fixed maturities: | | | | |
| U.S. government and government agencies and authorities | $ 57,622 | $1,832 | $  — | $ 59,454 |
| States, municipalities and political subdivisions | 38,587 | 947 | (282) | 39,252 |
| All other corporate | 12,008 | 113 | (34) | 12,087 |
| | 108,217 | 2,892 | (316) | 110,793 |
| | • • • • | | | |
| | $128,940 | $7,410 | $(316) | $136,034 |
| **1989** | | | | |
| Fixed maturities: | | | | |
| U.S. government and government agencies and authorities | $ 25,788 | $ 537 | $ (8) | $ 26,317 |
| States, municipalities and political subdivisions | 57,369 | 992 | (608) | 57,753 |
| All other corporate | 4,005 | 93 | — | 4,098 |
| | 87,162 | 1,622 | (616) | 88,168 |
| | • • • • | | | |
| | $110,384 | $5,585 | $(627) | $115,342 |
| | • • • • | | | |

The maturity distribution of fixed maturities at December 31, 1990 was as follows:

| (in thousands) | Cost | Market Value |
|---|---|---|
| Due in one year or less | $ 4,028 | $ 4,044 |
| Due after one year through five years | 51,492 | 52,727 |
| Due after five years through ten years | 45,332 | 46,545 |
| Due after ten years | 7,365 | 7,477 |
| | $108,217 | $110,793 |

78

The components of net investment income and realized investment gains for the years ended December 31 were as follows:

| (in thousands) | 1990 | 1989 | 1988 |
|---|---|---|---|
| • • • • | | | |
| Realized investment gains (losses): | | | |
| Fixed maturities: | | | |
| Gross gains | $ 49 | $ 5 | $ — |
| Gross losses | (485) | — | — |
| | (436) | 5 | — |
| • • • • | | | |
| Net realized investment gains | $ 442 | $218 | $323 |

The proceeds from the sales of fixed maturities were $17,552,000 for 1990. There were no sales of fixed maturities for 1989 and 1988.


AVEMCO CORPORATION, DECEMBER 31, 1990

*AVEMCO Corporation and Subsidiaries*
*Notes to Consolidated Financial Statements*

December 31, 1990

Summary of Significant Accounting Policies

• • • •

(e) Investments

Investments in fixed maturities (bonds and redeemable preferred stock) are carried at amortized cost. Fixed maturities are intended to be held until their maturity unless market and economic conditions dictate otherwise....

Gain or loss on securities transactions are recognized as realized or when permanent impairment occurs and are determined by the identified certificate method....

2. Investments

The following summarizes the amortized cost, unrealized gains and losses, and market value of investments in fixed income securities at December 31, 1990, 1989, and 1988. Bonds consist primarily of debt securities issued by states and political subdivisions.

| | Amortized Cost | Unrealized Gains | Losses | Market Value |
|---|---|---|---|---|
| December 31, 1990: | | | | |
| Bonds | $107,893,000 | $4,734,000 | $ 658,000 | $111,969,000 |
| Redeemable preferred stocks | 438,000 | 35,000 | — | 473,000 |
| Total | $108,331,000 | $4,769,000 | $ 658,000 | $112,442,000 |

*Investments (continued)*

|  | Amortized Cost | Unrealized Gains | Unrealized Losses | Market Value |
|---|---|---|---|---|
| **December 31, 1989:** | | | | |
| Bonds | $101,956,000 | $3,163,000 | $ 465,000 | $104,654,000 |
| Redeemable preferred stocks | 1,402,000 | 189,000 | 17,000 | 1,574,000 |
| Total | $103,358,000 | $3,352,000 | $ 482,000 | $106,228,000 |
| **December 31, 1988:** | | | | |
| Bonds | $ 92,479,000 | $2,388,000 | $1,146,000 | $ 93,721,000 |
| Redeemable preferred stocks | 2,522,000 | 123,000 | 65,000 | 2,580,000 |
| Total | $ 95,001,000 | $2,511,000 | $1,211,000 | $ 96,301,000 |

Below are the unrealized increases (decreases) in the market value of investments in fixed income securities for the years ended December 31, 1990, 1989 and 1988:

|  | 1990 | 1989 | 1988 |
|---|---|---|---|
| Bonds | $1,378,000 | $1,456,000 | $(917,000) |
| Redeemable preferred stocks | (137,000) | 114,000 | 16,000 |
| Net increase (decrease) | $1,241,000 | $1,570,000 | $(901,000) |

The amortized cost and market value of fixed income securities at December 31, 1990, by contractual maturities, are shown below. Expected maturities will differ from contractual maturities because borrowers may have the right to call or prepay obligations with or without call or prepayment penalties.

|  | December 31, 1990 | |
|---|---|---|
| Maturity | Amortized Cost | Market Value |
| Less than one year | $ 3,675,000 | $ 3,714,000 |
| 1 to 3 years | 13,428,000 | 13,771,000 |
| 3 to 5 years | 15,621,000 | 16,297,000 |
| 5 to 10 years | 43,584,000 | 45,578,000 |
| Over 10 years | 32,023,000 | 33,082,000 |
|  | $108,331,000 | $112,442,000 |

•  •  •  •

Realized gains (losses), before taxes, on the sale of investment securities are as follows for the years ended December 31, 1990, 1989, and 1988:

|  | 1990 | 1989 | 1988 |
|---|---|---|---|
| Fixed maturities | $ (40,000) | $ 96,000 | $ 262,000 |

•  •  •  •

|  | | | |
|---|---|---|---|
| Net realized gains (losses) | $1,969,000 | $2,686,000 | $(168,000) |

Proceeds from the sale and maturity of fixed income securities during 1990, 1989 and 1988, were $36,502,000, $30,292,000, and $14,143,000, respectively. Gross gains of $243,000, $266,000, and $457,000 in 1990, 1989 and 1988, respectively, and gross losses of $283,000, $170,000, and $195,000, in 1990, 1989 and 1988, respectively, were realized from these transactions.

CHUBB CORPORATION, DECEMBER 31, 1990

*Notes to Consolidated Financial Statements*

(1) Summary of Significant Accounting Policies

•• ••

(b) Investments

Short term investments, which have an original maturity of one year or less, are carried at amortized cost, which approximates market value. Fixed maturities, which include bonds and redeemable preferred stocks, are carried at amortized cost....

Fixed maturities are purchased to support the investment strategies of the Corporation, which are developed based on many factors including rate of return, maturity, credit risk, tax considerations and regulatory requirements. The Corporation has the ability to hold such securities to maturity and, subject to its investment strategies, intends to hold them until maturity. Market values for fixed maturities noted parenthetically on the balance sheets are principally a function of current interest rates. Care should be used in evaluating the significance of these estimated market values. The difference between amortized cost and the estimated market value of these investments is not reflected in the financial statements.

Realized gains and losses on the sale of investments are determined on the basis of the cost of the specific investments sold and are credited or charged to income....

•• ••

(2) Invested Assets and Related Income

•• ••

(b) Realized investment gains and losses were as follows:

| | Years Ended December 31 | | |
| | 1990 | 1989 | 1988 |
|---|---|---|---|
| *(in thousands)* | | | |
| Gross realized investment gains | | | |
| Fixed maturities | $ 51,156 | $ 25,993 | $ 26,851 |
| •• •• | | | |
| | 112,585 | 81,772 | 47,451 |
| Gross realized investment losses | | | |
| Fixed maturities | 27,200 | 25,259 | 47,879 |

•• ••

|  | Years Ended December 31 | | |
| --- | --- | --- | --- |
| *(in thousands)* | 1990 | 1989 | 1988 |
|  | 66,268 | 34,830 | 65,438 |
| Realized investment gains (losses) | 46,317 | 46,942 | (17,987) |
| Income tax (credit) | 16,124 | 16,010 | (5,028) |
|  | $ 30,193 | $ 30,932 | $(12,959) |

•••••

(d)  The amortized cost and estimated market value of fixed maturities at December, 31, 1990 were as follows:

| *(in thousands)* | Gross Amortized Cost | Gross Unrealized Gains | Estimated Unrealized Losses | Market Value |
| --- | --- | --- | --- | --- |
| Tax exempt | $3,739,710 | $ 97,882 | $16,792 | $3,820,800 |
| Taxable |  |  |  |  |
| U.S. Government and government agency and authority obligations | 957,743 | 10,493 | 3,274 | 964,962 |
| Foreign bonds | 429,357 | 3,356 | 10,565 | 422,148 |
| Corporate bonds | 1,261,653 | 27,686 | 32,645 | 1,256,694 |
| Mortgage-backed securities | 824,373 | 12,530 | 10,638 | 826,265 |
| Redeemable preferred stocks | 7,851 | 1,498 | 180 | 9,169 |
| Total taxable | 3,480,977 | 55,563 | 57,302 | 3,479,238 |
|  | $7,220,687 | $153,445 | $74,094 | $7,300,038 |

The change in unrealized appreciation or depreciation of fixed maturities was depreciation of $64,410,000, appreciation of $198,247,000 and depreciation of $64,161,000 for the years ended December 31, 1990, 1989 and 1988, respectively.

The amortized cost and estimated market value of fixed maturities at December 31, 1990 by contractual maturity were as follows:

| *(in thousands)* | Amortized Cost | Estimated Market Value |
| --- | --- | --- |
| Due in one year or less | $ 276,385 | $ 275,793 |
| Due after one year through five years | 1,478,069 | 1,501,200 |
| Due after five years through ten years | 2,437,910 | 2,462,545 |
| Due after ten years | 2,203,950 | 2,234,235 |
|  | 6,396,314 | 6,473,773 |
| Mortgage-backed securities | 824,373 | 826,265 |
|  | $7,220,687 | $7,300,038 |

•••

CIGNA CORPORATION, DECEMBER 31, 1990

*Notes to Financial Statements*

Note 1—Summary of Significant Accounting Policies

B) New Accounting Pronouncements:

•••

Also, in the fourth quarter of 1990, CIGNA adopted Statement of Position (SOP) 90-11, "Disclosure of Certain Information by Financial Institutions about Debt Securities Held as Assets," issued by the Accounting Standards Executive Committee of the American Institute of Certified Public Accountants. SOP 90-11 requires certain disclosures for debt securities held as assets and accounted for at other than market value.

In accordance with the provisions of these pronouncements, disclosures are presented throughout the Notes to Financial Statements as appropriate.

•••

C) Investments: Investments in fixed maturities include bonds and redeemable preferred stocks that are carried principally at amortized cost since CIGNA generally holds these investments until maturity and does not actively trade such investments for the purpose of maximizing short-term profits. Market values provided for fixed maturities are based on published market values, if available, or estimates by management....

....Realized gains and losses are reported as a component of revenues based upon specific identification of the investment assets. When impairment of the value of an investment is considered other than temporary, the decrease in value is reported as a realized investment loss and a new carrying value is established....

•••

Note 3-Investments

A) Valuation of Investments: Market value, cost and amortized cost of investments in fixed maturities and equity securities at December 31 were as follows:

| (*in millions*) | 1990 | 1989 |
| --- | --- | --- |
| Fixed maturities: | | |
| Carrying value and amortized cost | $22,965 | $21,467 |
| Market value | 23,656 | 22,344 |

•••

B) Fixed Maturities: Fixed maturities are generally intended to be held to maturity; therefore, care should be exercised in drawing any conclusions from market value information. The amortized cost and market value by maturity periods for these investments as of December 31, 1990 were as follows:

| (in millions) | Amortized Cost | Market Value |
|---|---|---|
| Due in one year or less | $ 906 | $ 943 |
| Due after one year through five years | 4,421 | 4,544 |
| Due after five years through ten years | 6,706 | 6,917 |
| Due after ten years | 7,550 | 7,779 |
|  | 19,583 | 20,183 |
| Mortgage-backed securities | 3,382 | 3,473 |
| Total | $22,965 | $23,656 |

The net unrealized appreciation on fixed maturities was $691 million and $877 million at December 31, 1990 and 1989, respectively. The increase (decrease) in the net unrealized appreciation on fixed maturities was ($186) million, $754 million and ($2) million in 1990, 1989 and 1988, respectively. These unrealized amounts are not reflected in the financial statements and are computed based on estimated market values before policyholders' share.

The gross unrealized appreciation (depreciation) for fixed maturities by investment category at December 31, 1990 was as follows:

| (in millions) | Amortized Cost | Appreciation | Depreciation | Market Value |
|---|---|---|---|---|
| Federal government bonds | $ 1,705 | $ 155 | $ (12) | $ 1,848 |
| State and local government bonds | 3,459 | 180 | (132) | 3,507 |
| Foreign government bonds | 1,373 | 47 | (49) | 1,371 |
| Corporate bonds | 11,548 | 614 | (283) | 11,879 |
| Mortgage-backed securities | 3,382 | 132 | (41) | 3,473 |
| Other | 1,498 | 138 | (58) | 1,578 |
| Total | $22,965 | $1,266 | $(575) | $23,656 |

••••

Note 4—Investment Income and Gains and Losses

B) Realized Investment Gains and Losses: Realized gains and losses on investments for the year ended December 31 were as follows:

| (in millions) | 1990 | 1989 | 1988 |
|---|---|---|---|
| Realized gains (losses): |  |  |  |
| Fixed maturities | $(37) | $ 13 | $13 |

••••

| | | | |
|---|---|---|---|
|  | (20) | 159 | 15 |
| Income taxes (benefits) | (5) | 55 | 7 |
| Net realized gains (losses) | $(15) | $104 | $ 8 |

Impairments in the value of investments that are other than temporary are included in realized gains and losses, and were $52 million, $8 million and $13 million in 1990, 1989 and 1988, respectively.

••••

Proceeds from voluntary sales of investments in fixed maturities were $3.2 billion, $2.2 billion and $1.9 billion in 1990, 1989 and 1988, respectively. Realized gains on such sales were $60 million, $55 million and $60 million for 1990, 1989 and 1988, respectively, and realized losses were $69 million, $35 million and $43 million, respectively.

## CNA FINANCIAL CORPORATION, DECEMBER 31, 1990

*CNA Financial Corporation*
*Notes to Financial Statements*

Note A. Significant Accounting Policies:

• • • •

Valuation of investments—Fixed maturities (bonds and redeemable preferred stocks) are generally carried at amortized cost....

Investment gains and losses—Realized investment gains and losses are determined on the basis of the cost of the specific securities sold. Investments with permanent loss in value are written down to estimated realizable values resulting in losses that are charged to income....

Note B. Investments:

• • • •

Analysis of Investment Gains (Losses)

| Year Ended December 31<br>(*in thousands of dollars*) | 1990 | 1989 | 1988 |
|---|---|---|---|
| Realized investment gains (losses):<br>Fixed maturities | $104,107 | $141,739 | $221,537 |

• • • •

| | | | |
|---|---|---|---|
| Net realized investing gains<br>  (losses) | (29,627) | 145,944 | 141,987 |

• • • •

Proceeds from sales of investments in fixed maturities securities during 1990 were $22.8 billion. Total realized investment gains of $284.3 million and losses of $180.2 million were recognized on sales of fixed maturities securities for the year ended December 31, 1990.

Summary of Investment in Fixed Maturities

| (*in thousands of dollars*) | Amortized Cost | Unrealized Gains | Unrealized Losses | Market Value |
|---|---|---|---|---|
| **December 31, 1990** | | | | |
| United States Treasury securities and obligations of government agencies | $ 2,848,284 | $ 15,991 | $ 6,337 | $ 2,857,938 |
| Mortgage-backed securities | 2,269,480 | 51,605 | 4,368 | 2,316,717 |
| States, municipalities and political subdivisions— tax exempt | 7,984,453 | 348,920 | 42,409 | 8,291,054 |
| Corporate securities | 1,293,297 | 41,587 | 156,958 | 1,177,926 |
| Other debt securities | 474,809 | 8,918 | 10,729 | 472,998 |
| Redeemable preferred stocks | 156,664 | 4,673 | 19,929 | 141,408 |
| Total fixed maturities | $15,027,077 | $471,694 | $240,730 | $15,258,041 |
| **December 31, 1989** | | | | |
| United States Treasury securities and obligations of government agencies | $ 382,566 | $ 5,586 | $ 1,920 | $ 386,232 |
| Mortgage-backed securities | 1,234,211 | 26,617 | 13,126 | 1,247,702 |
| States, municipalities and political subdivisions— tax exempt | 10,123,299 | 515,322 | 55,074 | 10,583,547 |
| Corporate securities | 929,028 | 26,818 | 64,070 | 891,776 |
| Other debt securities | 460,290 | 12,743 | 11,216 | 461,817 |
| Redeemable preferred stocks | 110,712 | 9,217 | 3,234 | 116,695 |
| Total fixed maturities | $13,240,106 | $596,303 | $148,640 | $13,687,769 |

The amortized cost and market value of fixed maturities at December 31, 1990, by contractual maturity, are shown below. Expected maturities will differ from contractual maturities because borrowers may have the right to call or prepay obligations with or without call or prepayment penalties. Mortgage-backed securities are grouped below based on the latest maturity date in the pool.

| | Amortized Cost | Market Value |
|---|---|---|
| Due in one year or less | $ 115,900 | $ 113,935 |
| Due after one year through five years | 756,182 | 755,458 |
| Due after five years through ten years | 3,843,766 | 3,821,890 |
| Due after ten years | 10,311,229 | $10,566,758 |
| | $15,027,077 | $15,258,041 |

••••

FIRST CENTRAL FINANCIAL CORPORATION, DECEMBER 31, 1990

*First Central Financial Corporation and Subsidiaries*
*Notes to Consolidated Financial Statements*

Note B—Significant Accounting Policies

•••

Investments: Fixed maturities (principally bonds and notes) are stated at cost, adjusted for amortization of premium or discount and other-than-temporary market value declines. The amortized cost of such investments differs from their market values; however, First Central had the ability and intent to hold these investments to maturity, at which time the full face value is expected to be realized.... Costs of investments disposed are determined under the first-in, first-out method....

•••

Note C—Investments

The major components of investments are summarized as follows:

|  | December 31 | |
|---|---|---|
|  | 1990 | 1989 |
| Fixed maturities: | | |
| U.S. Treasury notes | $ 299,554 | $ 599,460 |
| Obligations of states and political subdivisions | 24,450,028 | 24,984,771 |
| Debt securities issued by a foreign government | 481,000 | 430,000 |
| Corporate obligations | 6,419,175 | 6,691,171 |
| Total Fixed Maturities | $31,649,757 | $32,705,402 |

•••

At December 31, 1990, the amortized cost and estimated market values of investments in fixed maturities by categories of securities are as follows:

|  | Amortized Cost | Gross Unrealized Gains | Gross Unrealized Losses | Estimated Market Value |
|---|---|---|---|---|
| U.S. Treasury notes | $ 299,554 | $ 15,446 |  | $ 315,000 |
| Obligations of states and political subdivisions | 24,450,028 | 418,334 | $ 397,384 | 24,470,978 |
| Debt securities issued by a foreign government | 481,000 |  | 14,600 | 466,400 |
| Corporate obligations | 6,419,715 | 26,273 | 707,042 | 5,738,406 |
| Total | $31,649,757 | $460,053 | $1,119,026 | $30,990,784 |

The amortized cost and estimated market value of debt securities at December 31, 1990, by contractual maturity are shown below. Expected maturities will differ from contractual maturities because borrowers may have the right to call or prepay obligations with or without call or prepayment penalties.

|  | December 31, 1990 | |
|  | Amortized Cost | Estimated Market Value |
| --- | --- | --- |
| Due in one year or less | $ 879,325 | $ 882,438 |
| Due after one year through five years | 4,435,568 | 4,077,755 |
| Due after five years through ten years | 11,925,054 | 12,482,475 |
| Due after ten years through twenty years | 9,330,307 | 8,861,226 |
| Due after twenty years | 5,079,503 | 4,686,890 |
| Total | $31,649,757 | $30,990,784 |

• • • •

In 1990, 1989, and 1988, the proceeds from the sales of investments in fixed maturity securities carried at amortized cost were $2,955,828, $3,967,941, and $17,592,377, respectively. For 1990, 1989 and 1988, gross gains of $1,296, $39,630, and $71,217, respectively and gross losses of $63,080, $17,528, and $35,638, respectively, were realized on such sales.

The change in the difference between cost (principally amortized cost of bonds and notes) and market values for fixed maturities and equity securities for 1990, 1989, and 1988 is summarized below:

|  | Year Ended December 31 | | |
|  | 1990 | 1989 | 1988 |
| --- | --- | --- | --- |
| Fixed maturities: |  |  |  |
| Market value | $30,990,784 | $32,798,659 | $33,385,695 |
| Amortized cost | 31,649,757 | 32,705,402 | 34,015,902 |
| Unrealized Appreciation (Depreciation) at End of Year | (658,973) | 93,257 | (630,207) |
| Unrealized appreciation (depreciation) at beginning of year | 93,257 | (630,207) | (901,366) |
| Change in Unrealized Appreciation (Depreciation) | $ (752,230) | $ 723,464 | $ 271,159 |

• • • •

The major categories of net investment income are summarized as follows:

|  | Year Ended December 31 | | |
|  | 1990 | 1989 | 1988 |
| --- | --- | --- | --- |

• • • •

|  | | | |
| --- | --- | --- | --- |
| Realized gains (losses): |  |  |  |
| Fixed maturities | (61,784) | 22,102 | 36,019 |

88

| | Year Ended December 31 | | |
|---|---|---|---|
| | 1990 | 1989 | 1988 |
| | •••• | | |
| Net investment Income | $3,705,259 | $3,396,780 | $2,389,316 |

GAINSCO INC., DECEMBER 31, 1990

*Notes to Consolidated Financial Statements*
*December 31, 1990, 1989 and 1988*

(1)  Summary of Accounting Policies

•••• 

(b) Investments

Fixed maturities, principally bonds, are stated at amortized cost.... The "specific identification" method is used to determine costs of investments sold. Since investments are generally held until maturity or recovery of market value, provisions for possible losses are recorded only when the values have been permanently impaired. Realized capital gains on investments, before tax, have been reported in the consolidated statement of operations as a component of other income. The net realized loss for 1990 was $2,107 and the net realized gains for 1989 and 1988 were $8,479 and $219, respectively.

••••

(2) Investments

••••

Amortized Cost/Market Value of Investments in Debt Securities

The following schedule summarizes the amortized cost and estimated market values of investments in debt securities:

| (*in thousands*) | Amortized Cost | Gross Unrealized Gains | Gross Unrealized Losses | Estimated Market Value |
|---|---|---|---|---|
| Fixed Maturities: | | | | |
| US Government Securities - 1990 | $ 4,925 | 54 | (6) | 4,973 |
| US Government Securities - 1989 | 4,299 | 12 | (36) | 4,275 |
| US Government Securities - 1988 | 3,997 | — | (155) | 3,842 |
| Tax-exempt state & municipal bonds - 1990 | 55,070 | 662 | (52) | 55,680 |
| Tax-exempt state & municipal bonds - 1989 | 41,732 | 279 | (163) | 41,848 |
| Tax-exempt state & municipal bonds - 1988 | 24,815 | 51 | (344) | 24,522 |
| Other taxable fixed maturities - 1990 | 770 | — | (1) | 769 |

*Amortized Cost/Market Value of Investments in Debt Securities (continued)*

| (*in thousands*) | Amortized Cost | Gross Unrealized Gains | Gross Unrealized Losses | Estimated Market Value |
|---|---|---|---|---|
| Other taxable fixed maturities - 1989 | 1,000 | 3 | — | 1,003 |
| Other taxable fixed maturities - 1988 | 740 | 4 | — | 744 |
| Total Fixed Maturities - 1990 | $ 60,765 | 716 | (59) | 61,422 |
| Total Fixed Maturities - 1989 | 47,031 | 294 | (199) | 47,126 |
| Total Fixed Maturities - 1988 | 29,552 | 55 | (499) | 29,108 |

●●●●

Amortized Cost/Market Value of Debt Securities by Maturity 1990-89

The amortized cost and estimated market value of debt securities at December 31, 1990, by maturity, are shown below.

| | 1990 | | 1989 | |
|---|---|---|---|---|
| (*in thousands*) | Amortized Cost | Estimated Market Value | Amortized Cost | Estimated Market Value |
| Due in one year or less | $13,291 | 13,357 | 10,318 | 10,301 |
| Due after one year through five years | 39,892 | 40,380 | 31,946 | 31,978 |
| Due after five years through ten years | 7,062 | 7,158 | 4,333 | 4,411 |
| Due after ten years | 520 | 527 | 434 | 436 |
| | $60,765 | 61,422 | 47,031 | 47,126 |

| | 1988 | |
|---|---|---|
| (*in thousands*) | Amortized Cost | Estimated Market Value |
| Due in one year or less | 4,952 | 4,913 |
| Due after one year through five years | 22,561 | 22,241 |
| Due after five years through ten years | 1,861 | 1,781 |
| Due after ten years | 178 | 173 |
| | 29,552 | 29,108 |

●●●●

GEICO CORPORATION, DECEMBER 31, 1990

*GEICO Corporation*
*Notes to Consolidated Financial Statements*

●●●●

Note B: Significant Accounting Policies

••••

Investments

Investments in fixed maturities (bonds, notes and redeemable preferred stocks) are reported at amortized cost.... Realized gains and losses on sales of investments, as determined on a specific identification basis, are included in the statement of income....

Note D: Investment Operations

••••

Realized Gains (Losses)

Realized gains (losses) from sales of investments are summarized as follows:

| (*in thousands*) | 1990 | 1989 | 1988 |
|---|---|---|---|
| Fixed maturities | $ (4,964) | $  4,543 | $ 1,748 |

••••

| | | | |
|---|---|---|---|
| Realized gains | $19,587 | $109,133 | $82,351 |

Realized gains (losses) from sales of fixed maturities consist of gross realized gains of $2.3 million, $5.0 million and $4.1 million and gross realized losses of $7.2 million, $.4 million and $2.4 million for 1990, 1989 and 1988, respectively.

Unrealized Appreciation (Depreciation)

••••

Investments in fixed maturities are carried at amortized cost since such securities are generally held to maturity. A summary of unrealized appreciation (depreciation) on investments in fixed maturities is as follows:

| (*in thousands*) | 1990 | 1989 | 1988 |
|---|---|---|---|
| Market value | $1,941,535 | $1,693,351 | $1,684,156 |
| Amortized cost | 1,884,951 | 1,640,517 | 1,670,766 |
| Unrealized appreciation at December 31 | $   56,584 | $   52,834 | $   13,390 |
| Unrealized appreciation (depreciation) during the year | $    3,750 | $   39,444 | $  (15,654) |

Gross Unrealized Gains (Losses)

Gross unrealized gains (losses) on investments in fixed maturities are summarized as follows:

| (in thousands) | December 31, 1990 | December 31, 1989 |
|---|---|---|
| | 1990 | 1989 |
| Gross unrealized gains: | | |
| U.S. Treasury securities and obligations | | |
| of U.S. government corporations and agencies | $ 8,408 | $ 4,192 |
| Obligations of states and political | | |
| subdivisions | 46,151 | 46,852 |
| Corporate bonds and notes | 3,628 | 3,570 |
| Redeemable preferred stocks | 4,996 | 6,015 |
| | 63,183 | 60,629 |
| Gross unrealized losses: | | |
| U.S. Treasury securities and obligations | | |
| of U.S. government corporations and agencies | 1,222 | 680 |
| Obligations of states and political | | |
| subdivisions | 4,281 | 6,593 |
| Corporate bonds and notes | 741 | 270 |
| Redeemable preferred stocks | 355 | 252 |
| | 6,599 | 7,795 |
| | $56,584 | $52,834 |

• • • •

Investments in Fixed Maturities

The amortized cost and market value of investments in fixed maturities at December 31, 1990 are shown below by their maturity dates.

| (in thousands) | Amortized Cost | Market Value |
|---|---|---|
| 1991 | $ 117,504 | $ 118,078 |
| 1992-1995 | 699,443 | 717,477 |
| 1996-2000 | 576,668 | 595,037 |
| 2001 and after | 252,698 | 268,493 |
| Mortgage-backed securities | 238,638 | 242,450 |
| | $1,884,951 | $1,941,535 |

Mortgage-backed securities are primarily obligations of U.S. government corporations and agencies and have regular periodic principal repayments over the life of the issue.

# IV

## OTHER FINANCIAL INSTITUTIONS

Financial institutions other than banks and life or property and liability insurance enterprises also present information about debt securities in accordance with SOP 90-11. Examples of information disclosed in accordance with SOP 90-11 by twelve enterprises that operate primarily in these fields are presented below:

- Security brokerage (American Express Company, Merrill Lynch & Co., Inc.)

- Title insurance (Alleghany Corporation, First American Financial Corporation)

- Surety insurance (MBIA Inc.)

- Insurance agents and brokers (Argonaut Group Inc., Markel Corporation)

- Personal credit (Beneficial Corporation, Household International Inc., Primerica Corporation)

- Short-term business credit (Foothill Group Inc., Rochester Community Savings Bank)

The examples are classified alphabetically by company name.

ALLEGHANY CORPORATION, DECEMBER 31, 1990

*Notes to Consolidated Financial Statements*

1. Summary of Significant Accounting Principles

●●●●

b.  Investment Securities

Bonds and notes are carried at amortized cost based upon the ability and intent, as of each reporting date, to hold such investments for the foreseeable future, generally considered to be one year. Preferred stocks, other than those considered equity securities, and certificates of deposit, are carried at cost. A write-down of the carrying value is charged against earnings if evidence indicates a decline that is other than temporary in the underlying value and earning power of an individual investment security.

•  •  •  •

4.  Securities

Investment securities at December 31, 1990 and 1989 are summarized as follows (*in thousands*):

|  | 1990 | | 1989 | |
|---|---|---|---|---|
|  | Carrying Value | Market Value | Carrying Value | Market Value |
| Consolidated: |  |  |  |  |
| U.S. Government, government |  |  |  |  |
| agency and municipal obligations | $  641,797 | $  646,509 | $  429,190 | $  429,494 |
|  | •  •  •  • |  |  |  |
| Commercial paper | 82,580 | 82,580 | 140,459 | 140,459 |
|  | •  •  •  • |  |  |  |
| Bonds, notes and other | 322,261 | 320,139 | 241,246 | 239,955 |
|  | $1,257,055 | $1,259,629 | $1,186,887 | $1,238,006 |

•  •  •  •

The amortized cost and estimated market values of investments in debt securities at December 31, 1990 are summarized as follows (*in thousands*):

|  | Amortized Cost | Gross Unrealized Gains | Gross Unrealized Losses | Estimated Market Value |
|---|---|---|---|---|
| U.S. Government, government |  |  |  |  |
| agency and municipal obligations | $641,797 | $6,138 | $(1,426) | $646,509 |
| Commercial paper | 82,580 | — | — | 82,580 |
| Bonds, notes and other | 262,623 | 1,315 | (3,315) | 260,623 |
|  | $987,000 | $7,453 | $(4,741) | $989,712 |

The amortized cost and estimated market value of debt securities at December 31, 1990, by contractual maturity, are shown below. Expected maturities will differ from contractual maturities because borrowers may have the right to call or prepay obligations with or without call or prepayment penalties.

94

|                                          | Amortized Cost | Estimated Market Value |
|------------------------------------------|---------------:|-----------------------:|
| Due in one year or less                  | $349,634       | $349,976               |
| Due after one year through five years    | 361,822        | 363,954                |
| Due after five years through ten years   | 46,412         | 45,662                 |
| Due after ten years                      | 54,480         | 54,813                 |
|                                          | 812,348        | 814,405                |
| Mortgage-backed securities               | 174,652        | 175,307                |
|                                          | $987,000       | $989,712               |

The proceeds from sales of investments in debt securities were $131 million in 1990.

Gross realized gains and gross realized losses on sales of investments in debt securities were $61 million and $60 million, respectively, in 1990.

•••• 

AMERICAN EXPRESS COMPANY, DECEMBER 31, 1990

*Notes to Consolidated Financial Statements*

1.  Summary of Significant Accounting Policies

•••• 

Investments: Debt securities and investment mortgage loans, other than trading securities of SLB, are carried at amortized cost, except where there is a permanent impairment of value, in which case the investments are carried at estimated realizable value. The Company has the ability and, absent unforeseen circumstances, the intent to recover the costs of these investments by holding them until maturity.... mandatorily redeemable preferred stocks.... are carried at cost....

•••• 

7.  Investments

Investments carried at amortized cost are distributed by type and maturity as presented below. Annual yields related to state and municipal obligations and preferred stocks have been increased to reflect the tax equivalent basis at the U.S. statutory rate.

December 31, 1990

| *(dollars in millions)* | Cost | Market | Gross Unrealized Gains | Gross Unrealized Losses | Weighted Average Tax Equivalent Yield(*) |
|---|---:|---:|---|---|---|
| U.S. Government and agencies obligations |  |  |  |  |  |
| Due within 1 year | $ 174 | $ 174 |  |  |  |
| Due after 1 year through 5 years(**) | 35 | 36 |  |  |  |

*Investments (continued)*

| (dollars in millions) | Cost | Market | Gross Unrealized Gains | Gross Unrealized Losses | Weighted Average Tax Equivalent Yield(*) |
|---|---|---|---|---|---|
| Due after 5 years | | | | | |
| through 10 years | 40 | 41 | | | |
| Due after 10 years | 9 | 9 | | | |
| | 258 | 260 | $ 2 | $ — | 7.9% |
| State and municipal obligations | | | | | |
| Due within 1 year | 314 | 320 | | | |
| Due after 1 year | | | | | |
| through 5 years(**) | 1,328 | 1,383 | | | |
| Due after 5 years | | | | | |
| through 10 years | 2,541 | 2,623 | | | |
| Due after 10 years | 1,407 | 1,426 | | | |
| | 5,590 | 5,752 | 185 | 23 | 11.2% |
| Corporate bonds and obligations | | | | | |
| Due within 1 year | 2,830 | 2,810 | | | |
| Due after 1 year | | | | | |
| through 5 years(**) | 2,527 | 2,434 | | | |
| Due after 5 years | | | | | |
| through 10 years | 4,419 | 4,239 | | | |
| Due after 10 years | 1,648 | 1,630 | | | |
| | 11,424 | 11,113 | 178 | 489 | 9.1% |
| Foreign government obligations | | | | | |
| Due within 1 year | 238 | 235 | | | |
| Due after 1 year | | | | | |
| through 5 years(**) | 180 | 176 | | | |
| Due after 5 years | | | | | |
| through 10 years | 321 | 297 | | | |
| Due after 10 years | 30 | 27 | | | |
| | 769 | 735 | 5 | 39 | 9.7% |
| Mortgage-backed securities | 9,708 | 9,804 | 154 | 58 | 9.2% |
| Investment mortgage loans and other | 2,770 | 2,748 | 10 | 32 | 11.1% |
| Total | $30,519 | $30,412 | $534 | $641 | 9.7% |

December 31, 1989

| (dollars in millions) | Cost | Market | Weighted Average Tax Equivalent Yield(*) |
|---|---|---|---|
| **U.S. Government and agencies obligations** | | | |
| Due within 1 year | $ 157 | | |
| Due after 1 year through 5 years(**) | 217 | | |
| Due after 5 years through 10 years | | | |
| Due after 10 years | — | | |
| | 374 | $ 375 | 8.9% |
| **State and municipal obligations** | | | |
| Due within 1 year | 175 | | |
| Due after 1 year through 5 years(**) | 3,547 | | |
| Due after 5 years through 10 years | | | |
| Due after 10 years | 1,302 | | |
| | 5,024 | 5,174 | 11.4% |
| **Corporate bonds and obligations** | | | |
| Due within 1 year | 1,905 | | |
| Due after 1 year through 5 years(**) | 8,763 | | |
| Due after 5 years through 10 years | | | |
| Due after 10 years | 1,701 | | |
| | 12,369 | 11,647 | 8.6% |
| **Foreign government obligations** | | | |
| Due within 1 year | 174 | | |
| Due after 1 year through 5 years(**) | 802 | | |
| Due after 5 years through 10 years | | | |
| Due after 10 years | 30 | | |
| | 1,006 | 967 | 8.7% |
| Mortgage-backed securities | 7,707 | 8,302 | 9.5% |
| Investment mortgage loans and other | 2,602 | 2,610 | 11.2% |
| Total | $29,082 | $29,075 | 9.6% |

(*) Calculated on securities cost.
(**) For 1989, this caption also includes Due after 5 years through 10 years.

Notes: Proceeds from sales of investments held at cost during 1990 were $2,187 million. Gross gains and gross losses realized on those sales were immaterial. Mortgage-backed securities include GNMA, FNMA and FHLMC securities totaling $8,348 million in 1990 and $6,421 million in 1989.

*Argonaut Group, Inc. and Subsidiaries*
*Notes to Consolidated Financial Statements*

1. Summary of Significant Accounting Policies

•  •  •  •

Investments

Investments in fixed maturities include bonds, notes, and redeemable preferred stocks, valued at amortized cost and are generally held for long-term investment.... Gains and losses on sales of investments are computed on the specific identification method and are reflected in total revenue.

•  •  •  •

2. Investments

Gains on sales of investments for the years ended December 31, were as follows.

| (*in millions*) | 1990 | 1989 | 1988 |
|---|---|---|---|
| Fixed maturities | $0.4 | $(0.9) | $ (1.9) |
| Equity securities | 2.8 | 1.9 | 39.0 |
| | $3.2 | $ 1.0 | $37.1 |

•  •  •  •

The amortized cost and market values of fixed maturity investments as of December 31, 1990 are as follows.

| (*in millions*) | Amortized Cost | Gross Unrealized Gains | Gross Unrealized Losses | Market Value |
|---|---|---|---|---|
| U.S. Treasury securities | $ 901.2 | $17.7 | $ — | $ 918.9 |
| Obligations of states and political subdivisions | 389.0 | 9.8 | 1.4 | 397.4 |
| Corporate securities | 194.8 | 1.4 | 3.2 | 193.0 |
| Redemptive preferred stock | 44.3 | 0.7 | 1.4 | 43.6 |
| | $1,529.3 | $29.6 | $6.0 | $1,552.9 |

The amortized cost and market value of fixed maturity investments as of December 31, 1990, by contractual maturity, are shown below.

| (*in millions*) | Amortized Cost | Market Value |
|---|---|---|
| Due in one year or less | $ 209.4 | $ 210.6 |
| Due after one year through five years | 860.2 | 874.9 |
| Due after five years through ten years | 382.8 | 391.9 |
| Due after ten years | 76.9 | 75.5 |
| | $1,529.3 | $1,552.9 |

Proceeds from sales of fixed maturity investments during 1990 were $99.0 million. Gross gains of $1.0 million and gross losses of $(0.6) million were realized on those sales.

• • • •

Unrealized appreciation of fixed maturity investments increased $17.4 million in 1990, increased $31.5 million in 1989 and decreased $18.2 million in 1988. These amounts are not included in the financial statements.

• • • •

BENEFICIAL CORPORATION, DECEMBER 31, 1990

*Beneficial Corporation and Subsidiaries*
*Notes to Financial Statements*
(*in millions, except per share amounts*)

1. Summary of Significant Accounting Principles and Practices

• • • •

d) Valuation of Investments.

Debt securities are carried at amortized cost...

4. Investments

The amortized cost and estimated market values of investments in debt securities at December 31, 1990 are as follows:

| | Carrying Amount | Gross Unrealized Gains | Gross Unrealized Losses | Market Value |
|---|---|---|---|---|
| Debt Securities: | | | | |
| Municipal | $ 83.7 | $ .8 | $ (5.4) | $ 79.1 |
| Corporate | 290.5 | 3.1 | (5.6) | 288.0 |
| U.S. Government | 58.2 | 1.0 | (.2) | 59.0 |
| Commercial Paper | 13.1 | — | — | 13.1 |
| Other | 33.9 | .2 | — | 34.1 |
| Total | $479.4 | $5.1 | $(11.2) | $473.3 |

The amortized cost and estimated market value of debt securities at December 31, 1990, by contractual maturity are shown below. Expected maturities will differ from contractual maturities because borrowers may have the right to call or prepay obligations with or without call or prepayment penalties.

|                                        | Carrying Amount | Market Value |
|----------------------------------------|-----------------|--------------|
| Due in one year or less                | $ 32.2          | $ 33.2       |
| Due after one year through five years  | 55.1            | 82.8         |
| Due after five years through ten years | 165.8           | 148.5        |
| Due after ten years                    | 226.3           | 208.8        |
| Total                                  | $479.4          | $473.3       |

The amortized cost of debt securities at December 31, 1989 was $365.4, and the estimated market value was $363.8.

Proceeds from sales of debt securities during 1990 were $1,208.9. Gross gains of $2.1 and gross losses of $.2 were realized on those sales.

•••• 

FIRST AMERICAN FINANCIAL CORPORATION, DECEMBER 31, 1990

*Notes to Consolidated Financial Statements*

The First American Financial Corporation and Subsidiary Companies

Note 3.

Debt Securities:

The amortized cost and estimated market value of investments in debt securities are as follows:

| (*in thousands*)                        | Amortized Cost | Gross Unrealized Gains | Gross Unrealized Losses | Estimated Market Value |
|-----------------------------------------|----------------|------------------------|-------------------------|------------------------|
| 1990                                    |                |                        |                         |                        |
| U.S. Treasury securities                | $28,575        | $ 573                  | $(217)                  | $28,931                |
| Obligations of states and political subdivisions | 40,822 | 1,229            | (720)                   | 41,331                 |
| Mortgage-backed securities and other    | 12,247         | 211                    | (59)                    | 12,399                 |
|                                         | $81,644        | $2,013                 | $(996)                  | $82,661                |
| 1989                                    |                |                        |                         |                        |
| U.S. Treasury securities                | $27,656        | $ 276                  | $(326)                  | $27,606                |
| Obligations of states and political subdivisions | 40,029 | 766              | (335)                   | 40,460                 |
| Mortgage-backed securities and other    | 5,093          | 126                    | (252)                   | 4,967                  |
|                                         | $72,778        | $1,168                 | $(913)                  | $73,033                |

The amortized cost and estimated market value of debt securities at December 31, 1990, by contractual maturities are as follows:

| (*in thousands*) | Amortized Cost | Estimated Market Value |
|---|---|---|
| Due in one year or less | $12,742 | $12,842 |
| Due after one year through five years | 33,900 | 34,410 |
| Due after five years through ten years | 15,364 | 15,631 |
| Due after ten years | 8,472 | 8,463 |
| | 70,478 | 71,346 |
| Mortgage-backed securities | 11,166 | 11,315 |
| | $81,644 | $82,661 |

Unrealized gains and losses on debt securities are not recognized because management intends to hold the investments long-term or until maturity. Realized gains and losses were not significant for the three years ended December 31, 1990.

FOOTHILL GROUP INC., DECEMBER 31, 1990

*The Foothill Group, Inc.*
*Notes to Consolidated Financial Statements*

December 31, 1990

Note 1. Summary of Significant Accounting Policies

•••

Basis of Presentation

In 1990, the Company .... adopted Statement of Position 90-11 which requires disclosures about debt instruments held as assets. Certain reclassifications have been made to prior year amounts to conform to the 1990 presentation.

•••

Investments

Investments consist primarily of corporate marketable debt securities and are carried at cost, adjusted for amortization of premiums, accretion of discounts and estimated permanent impairments in value. Current market values of investments are estimated by the Company's management based on available market quotations, which are generally available only from a limited number of dealers (or, for some securities, are not available) and may not represent firm bids of such dealers or prices for actual sales. Market values were approximately $16,985,000 and $52,736,000, which were $944,000 and $7,876,000 less than carrying value at December 31, 1990 and 1989, respectively. At December 31, 1990 and 1989, gross unrealized gains were $1,195,000 and $3,827,000, respectively, and gross unrealized losses were $2,139,000 and $11,703,000, respectively. The Company has recorded valuation adjustments in cases where permanent impairment in estimated net realizable value below the Company's cost basis in these non-investment grade investments is believed to have occured. Further impairments in value of these securities, which might be evidenced by continued deterioration in their market value, could require the Company to record additional valuation adjustments to reflect the expected net realizable value of the securities. During 1990, the Company experienced significant erosion in the portfolio value and recorded $16,214,000 in valuation adjustments and losses. Included in the financial statements are gross realized gains of $2,406,000 and gross realized losses of $3,999,000 resulting from sales of investments whose gross sales proceeds totalled $32,442,000. Included in these proceeds are cash proceeds of $29,602,000, as shown in the Statement of Cash Flows, and noncash proceeds of $2,840,000 ($2,047,000 in 1989), which resulted from investment reorganizations or exchanges. There were no significant net gains resulting from these debt exchange transactions in 1990.

•••

The approximate contractual maturities of investments, at adjusted cost and related estimated market value are as follows:

|  | Estimated Market Value | Carrying Value |
|---|---|---|
| 1991 | $2,122,000 | $2,122,000 |
| 1992-1995 | 4,594,000 | 4,926,000 |
| 1996-2000 | 8,569,000 | 9,241,000 |
| Thereafter | 1,700,000 | 1,640,000 |

•••

HOUSEHOLD INTERNATIONAL INC., DECEMBER 31, 1990

*Household International, Inc. and Subsidiaries*
*Notes to Financial Statements*

1. Summary of Significant Accounting Policies

•••

Investments

The investment securities portfolio is comprised of debt securities, equity securities, and mortgage and policyholder loans. These securities are intended to be held for the foreseeable future. Investment securities generally are carried at cost or amortized cost except that marketable equity securities held by the company's insurance subsidiaries are carried at market values. Cost of investment securities sold generally is determined using the first-in, first-out ("FIFO") method. Accrued investment income is classified with investments.

•••

2. Investment Securities

Investment securities at December 31 were as follows (*millions of dollars*):

|  | 1990 | | | 1989 | | |
|---|---|---|---|---|---|---|
|  | Cost | Market | Carrying Value | Cost | Market | Carrying Value |
| •••| | | | | | |
| Other: | | | | | | |
| Corporate bonds | 2,511.3 | 2,415.4 | 2,511.3 | 2,446.5 | 2,440.1 | 2,446.5 |
| Government bonds | 977.5 | 985.0 | 977.5 | 493.1 | 494.1 | 493.1 |

|  | 1990 | | | 1989 | | |
|---|---|---|---|---|---|---|
|  | Cost | Market | Carrying Value | Cost | Market | Carrying Value |
|  | | | •••• | | | |
| Commercial paper | 370.6 | 371.9 | 370.6 | 245.6 | 244.4 | 245.6 |
|  | | | •••• | | | |
| Total investment securities | | $5,122.3 | $5,106.2 | | $4,148.0 | $4,138.1 |

The investment portfolio, exclusive of marketable equity securities, had at December 31, 1990 and 1989 gross unrealized gains of $58 and $62.9 million and gross unrealized losses of $145.1 and $69.5 million, respectively .... Proceeds from sales of investments carried at amortized cost during 1990 were $668.5 million. Gross gains of $11.2 million and gross losses of $9.2 million were realized on those sales. Investment income, including net realized gains (losses), for 1990, 1989 and 1988 was $425.9, $364.4, and $253.0 million, respectively.

.... At December 31, 1990 contractual maturities of investments carried at amortized cost and estimated market value were as follows.

(*millions of dollars*):

|  | Estimated Cost | Market Value |
|---|---|---|
| Within 1 year | $ 716.0 | $ 716.7 |
| Over 1 but within 5 years | 948.1 | 937.8 |
| Over 5 but within 10 years | 2,023.2 | 1,955.3 |
| Over 10 years | 1,243.3 | 1,233.7 |
|  | $4,930.6 | $4,843.5 |

••••

MARKEL CORPORATION, DECEMBER 31, 1990

*Notes to Consolidated Financial Statements*

1. Summary of Significant Accounting Policies

••••

b) Investments

Investments in securities with fixed maturities are carried at amortized cost. The Company has the ability to hold its fixed maturities to maturity and, at December 31, 1990, has no intent of disposing of any specific fixed maturity investments prior to maturity.... Realized gains and losses on sales of investments are based on the cost of the securities sold determined on a first-in, first-out basis....

3. Investments

••••

d) The following table presents an analysis of the Company's realized and unrealized gains and losses on investments (*dollars in thousands*):

|  | Years ended December 31, | | |
| --- | --- | --- | --- |
|  | 1990 | 1989 | 1988 |
| **Realized gains:** | | | |
| Fixed maturities | $ 52 | $ 405 | $ 112 |
| Equity securities | 638 | 1,562 | 696 |
|  | 690 | 1,967 | 808 |
| **Realized losses:** | | | |
| Fixed maturities | 638 | 89 | 200 |
| Equity securities | 568 | 154 | 134 |
|  | 1,206 | 243 | 334 |
| Net realized gains (losses) from sales of investments | $ (516) | $1,724 | $ 474 |
| Unrealized gains (losses) during the year: | | | |
| Fixed maturities | $ 1,613 | $ 405 | $ (217) |
| Equity securities | $(2,775) | $ (145) | 1,205 |
| Net increase (decrease) | (1,162) | $ 260 | $ 988 |

e) The amortized cost and estimated market value of fixed maturities at December 31, 1990 were as follows (*dollars in thousands*):

|  | Amortized Cost | Gross Unrealized Gains | Gross Unrealized Losses | Estimated Market Value |
| --- | --- | --- | --- | --- |
| U.S. Treasury securities and obligations of U.S. government agencies | $ 21,621 | $ 359 | $ (18) | $ 21,962 |
| Obligations of states and political subdivisions | 61,770 | 811 | (268) | 62,313 |
| Corporate securities | 121,174 | 474 | (8,370) | 113,278 |
| Mortgage backed securities | 13,410 | 13 | (97) | 13,326 |
| Other debt securities | 13,991 | 30 | (297) | 13,724 |
| Totals | $231,966 | $1,687 | $(9,050) | $224,603 |

f) The amortized cost and estimated market value of fixed maturities at December 31, 1990, by contractual maturity, are shown below. Expected maturities may differ from contractual maturities because borrowers may have the right to call or prepay obligations with or without call or prepayment penalties (*dollars in thousands*).

|                                        | Amortized Cost | Estimated Market Value |
|----------------------------------------|----------------|------------------------|
| Due in one year or less                | $ 12,869       | $ 12,882               |
| Due after one year through five years  | 74,385         | 72,332                 |
| Due after five years through ten years | 59,144         | 57,056                 |
| Due after ten years                    | 85,568         | 82,333                 |
| Totals                                 | $231,966       | $224,603               |

••••

MBIA INC., DECEMBER 31, 1990

*MBIA Inc. and Subsidiaries*
*Notes to Consolidated Financial Statements*

2.  Significant Accounting Policies

••••

Investments

Fixed maturity securities which the Company intends to hold until maturity are classified as investments and are therefore carried at amortized cost. Bond discounts and premiums are amortized on the effective-yield method over the remaining term of the securities. For prerefunded bonds the remaining term is determined based on the contractual refunding date. Short-term investments are carried at amortized cost, which approximates market value. Realized gains or losses on sale of investments are determined by specific identification and are included in net investment income. Investment income is recorded as earned.

••••

6.  Investments

••••

The table below sets forth the book value composition of the consolidated investment portfolio of the Company as of December 31, 1990 and 1989.

Investment Category

| (*in thousands*)                             | 1990       | 1989       |
|----------------------------------------------|------------|------------|
| Fixed maturities                             |            |            |
| Taxable bonds                                |            |            |
| United States Treasury and Government Agency | $ 342,635  | $ 228,748  |
| Corporate and other obligations              | 184,039    | 108,212    |
| Tax-exempt bonds                             |            |            |
| State and municipal obligations              | 1,107,768  | 1,081,165  |
| Total fixed maturities                       | 1,634,442  | 1,418,125  |

*Investments (continued)*

| (*in thousands*) | 1990 | 1989 |
|---|---|---|
| Short-term investments | 68,242 | 60,020 |
| Other investments | 21,777 | 22,707 |
| Total investments | $1,724,461 | $1,500,852 |
| Market value as a percentage of amortized cost of fixed maturities | 101.0% | 99.9% |

•  •  •  •

The table below sets forth the distribution by maturity of fixed maturities and short-term investments at amortized cost and market value as of December 31, 1990.

| Maturity (*in thousands*) | Amortized Cost | Market Value |
|---|---|---|
| Within 1 year | $  68,242 | $  68,242 |
| Beyond 1 year but within 5 years | 420,089 | 415,877 |
| Beyond 5 years but within 10 years | 389,490 | 393,346 |
| Beyond 10 years but within 15 years | 337,006 | 343,902 |
| Beyond 15 years but within 20 years | 234,151 | 239,257 |
| Beyond 20 years | 253,706 | 258,526 |
| Total fixed maturities and short-term investments | $1,702,684 | $1,719,150 |

7.  Investment Income and Gains and Losses

•  •  •  •

The change in net unrealized gains (losses) consists of:

| | Years ended December 31 | | |
|---|---|---|---|
| (*in thousands*) | 1990 | 1989 | 1988 |
| Fixed maturities | $18,375 | $36,232 | $(8,558) |
| Other investments | (4,228) | 1,389 | — |
| Total | 14,147 | 37,621 | (8,558) |
| Deferred income taxes (benefit) | (472) | 472 | — |
| Unrealized gains (losses)—net | $14,619 | $37,149 | $(8,558) |

Unrealized gains (losses) consist of:

| (*in thousands*) | As of December 31 | | |
| --- | --- | --- | --- |
| | 1990 | 1989 | 1988 |
| Fixed maturities: | | | |
| Gains | $23,825 | $ 15,190 | $    264 |
| Losses | (7,359) | (17,099) | (38,405) |
| Net | 16,466 | (1,909) | (38,141) |
| Other investments: | | | |
| Gains (losses) | (2,839) | 1,389 | — |
| Total | 13,627 | (520) | (38,141) |
| Deferred income taxes | — | 472 | — |
| Unrealized gains (losses)—net | $13,627 | $  ( 992) | $(38,141) |

MERRILL LYNCH & CO. INC., DECEMBER 31, 1990

*Notes to Consolidated Financial Statements*
*(Dollars in Thousands, Except Per Share Amounts)*

Summary of Significant Accounting Policies

• • • •

Security Transactions

• • • •

Investment securities include equity and long-term debt instruments other than those held for sale in the normal course of business... Debt investment securities are carried at amortized cost unless a decline in value is deemed other than temporary in which case the carrying value of the investment is adjusted. Amortization of premium or discount as well as any unrealized losses deemed other than temporary are reflected in earnings of the current period.

• • • •

Insurance

• • • •

Investments held by insurance subsidiaries in debt securities and redeemable preferred stock are carried at amortized cost unless a decline in value is deemed other than temporary, in which case the carrying value is adjusted....

Insurance Operations

• • • •

The estimated market value of investments held by insurance subsidiaries as of December 28,

1990 and December 29, 1989 was $8,554,713 and $7,579,712, respectively. Additional information regarding investments of insurance subsidiaries as of December 28, 1990 follows:

| | Carrying Value | Gross Unrealized Gains | Gross Unrealized Losses | Estimated Market Value |
|---|---|---|---|---|
| Corporate securities | $4,370,626 | $22,995 | $(146,519) | $4,247,102 |
| Mortgage-backed securities | 3,264,323 | 53,784 | (10,483) | 3,307,624 |
| U.S. Treasury obligations | 68,342 | 1,784 | (1,060) | 69,066 |
| Obligations of states and political subdivisions | 35,117 | — | (3,563) | 31,554 |
| Debt securities issued by foreign governments | 18,749 | 235 | (197) | 18,787 |
| Total Debt Securities | 7,757,157 | 78,798 | (161,822) | 7,674,133 |
| Other Investments | 883,076 | 209 | (2,705) | 880,580 |
| Total | $8,640,233 | $79,007 | $(164,527) | $8,554,713 |

The carrying value and estimated market value of debt securities at December 28, 1990, by contractual maturity, are shown below. Expected maturities will differ from contractual maturities because borrowers may have the right to call or prepay obligations with or without call or prepayment penalties.

| | Carrying Value | Estimated Market Value |
|---|---|---|
| Due in one year or less | $ 121,559 | $ 121,526 |
| Due after one year through five years | 1,388,626 | 1,373,493 |
| Due after five years through ten years | 2,212,095 | 2,124,715 |
| Due after ten years | 770,554 | 746,775 |
| Subtotal | 4,492,834 | 4,366,509 |
| Mortgage-backed securities | 3,264,323 | 3,307,624 |
| Total | $7,757,157 | $7,674,133 |

Proceeds from sales of investments in debt securities during 1990 were $1,793,332. Gross gains of $24,152 and gross losses of $29,898 were realized on those sales.


PRIMERICA CORPORATION, DECEMBER 31, 1990

*Notes to Consolidated Financial Statements*
*(in millions of dollars except per share amounts)*

4. Fixed Maturities

The amortized cost and estimated market values of investments in fixed maturities (principally bonds, notes and redeemable preferred stocks) are as follows:

| December 31, 1990 | Amortized Cost | Gross Unrealized | | Estimated Market Value |
|---|---|---|---|---|
| | | Gains | Losses | |
| Mortgage-backed securities- principally obligations of U.S. Government agencies | $1,421.4 | $32.6 | $ (4.8) | $1,449.2 |
| U.S. Treasury securities and obligations of U.S. Government corporations and agencies | 252.2 | 9.7 | (.2) | 261.7 |
| Obligations of states and political subdivisions | 48.5 | 1.9 | (.5) | 49.9 |
| Debt securities issued by foreign governments | 6.3 | — | (.1) | 6.2 |
| Corporate securities | 295.2 | 4.4 | (8.5) | 291.1 |
| Other debt securities | 248.5 | 4.3 | (2.7) | 250.1 |
| Totals | $2,272.1 | $52.9 | $(16.8) | $2,308.2 |

The amortized cost and estimated market value at December 31, 1990 by contractual maturity are shown below. Actual maturities will differ from contractual maturities because borrowers may have the right to call or prepay obligations with or without call or prepayment penalties.

| | Amortized Cost | Estimated Market Value |
|---|---|---|
| Due after one year through five years | $ 156.1 | $ 159.8 |
| Due after five years through ten years | 360.1 | 358.4 |
| Due after ten years | 334.5 | 340.8 |
| | 850.7 | 859.0 |
| Mortgage-backed securities | 1,421.4 | 1,449.2 |
| | $2,272.1 | $2,308.2 |

Gross after-tax gains of $7.0 (pre-tax $10.6) and gross after-tax losses of $9.5 (pre-tax $14.4) were realized from sales of investments in debt securities during 1990.


ROCHESTER COMMUNITY SAVINGS BANK, NOVEMBER 30, 1990

*The Rochester Community Savings Bank and Subsidiaries*
*Notes To Consolidated Financial Statements*
*November 30, 1990, 1989 and 1988*

1.  Accounting Policies

•  •  •  •

Investment Securities: Bonds are carried at amortized cost net of an allowance for possible losses. Provisions for possible losses are charged to operations based upon management's evaluation of potential losses in the bond portfolio. Discounts are accreted and premiums are amortized during the term of the underlying bond on a level-yield method unless there are call provisions. Premiums on bonds which are callable are amortized to the call date.

Gains or losses on sales of investment securities are recognized based on the specific identification method. It is the Bank's intent to hold its investment securities to maturity.

••••

3. Investment Securities

A summary of investment securities follows:

| November 30,<br>(in thousands) | 1990 | | 1989 | |
|---|---|---|---|---|
| | Carrying<br>Value | Market<br>Value | Carrying<br>Value | Market<br>Value |
| U.S. Government and its agencies'<br>obligations | $ 12,896 | $ 12,870 | $ 44,851 | $ 44,566 |
| State and municipal obligations | 4,920 | 4,321 | 10,723 | 9,956 |
| Corporate and other obligations: | | | | |
| Investment grade | 253,322 | 238,794 | 369,052 | 356,339 |
| Non-investment grade | 54,881 | 34,516 | 75,566 | 63,476 |
| Common stock | 1,791 | 1,019 | 1,791 | 1,047 |
| Preferred stock | 13,861 | 11,375 | 18,030 | 16,350 |
| | 341,671 | 302,895 | 520,013 | 491,734 |
| Less: | | | | |
| Allowance for bond portfolio | 3,403 | | 5,397 | |
| Unrealized depreciation on<br>marketable equity securities | 1,716 | | 1,091 | |
| | $336,552 | $302,895 | $ 13,525 | $491,734 |

A summary of bond maturities at amortized follows:

| (in thousands) | U.S.<br>Government<br>and its<br>Agencies | State<br>and<br>Municipal | Corporate<br>and<br>Other |
|---|---|---|---|
| November 30, 1990 | | | |
| Due within 1 year | $11,547 | $ — | $102,826 |
| Due in 1 to 5 years | 1,269 | — | 67,963 |
| Due in 5 to 10 years | 80 | 1,147 | 74,856 |
| Due after 10 years | — | 3,773 | 62,558 |
| | $12,896 | $ 4,920 | $308,203 |
| November 30, 1989 | | | |
| Due within 1 year | $16,856 | $ — | $ 64,552 |
| Due in 1 to 5 years | 27,903 | 1,961 | 194,936 |
| Due in 5 to 10 years | 92 | 3,230 | 107,288 |
| Due after 10 years | — | 5,532 | 77,842 |
| | $44,851 | $10,723 | $444,618 |

At November 30, 1990, the Bank had gross unrealized gains and gross unrealized losses of $109,000 and $35,627,000, respectively, on bonds....

# APPENDIX

## USING NAARS TO OBTAIN ADDITIONAL EXAMPLES OF INFORMATION ABOUT DEBT SECURITIES DISCLOSED IN ACCORDANCE WITH SOP 90-11

Readers of this survey who have access to the National Automated Accounting Research System (NAARS) can obtain additional examples of information about debt securities disclosed in accordance with SOP 90-11. They can do so by using the search frame that was used to obtain the examples presented in this survey. The following search frame was used to obtain those examples:

## FTNT (INVESTMENT OR DEBT OR MORTGAGE BACKED W/5 SECURITIES) AND SIC (>599 W/SEG <700)

Following those instructions, the computer presented notes to financial statements containing the words "investment" or "debt" or "mortgage backed" within five words of the word "securities." The phrase in the search frame following the word *AND* confined the financial statements to those for financial institutions, which have Security Industry Code numbers between 600 and 700.